Helen Fast

Beyond Integration

By the same authors

**The Family Inside:
Working with the Multiple**
(with Lynda Shirar)

A NORTON PROFESSIONAL BOOK

Beyond Integration

One Multiple's Journey

Doris Bryant

Judy Kessler

W.W. Norton & Company
New York   London

The poem on page 133 is from *Illuminations* by Stephen C. Paul, illustrated by Gary Max Collins. Text copyright © 1991 by Stephen C. Paul. Reprinted by permission of HarperCollins Publishers, Inc.

Printed in the United States of America

First Edition

Manufacturing by Haddon Craftsmen, Inc.

For information about permission to reproduce selections from this book, write to Permissions, W.W. Norton Company, Inc., 500 Fifth Avenue, New York, NY 10110

Library of Congress Cataloging-in-Publication Data

Bryant, Doris.
    Beyond integration : one multiple's journey / Doris Bryant and Judy Kessler.
        p.   cm.
    "A Norton professional book."
    Includes bibliographical references and index.
    ISBN 0-393-70206-5
    1. Kessler, Judy, 1950-   . 2. Multiple personality--Patients--Biography.   3. Multiple personality--Treatment--Case studies.
    I. Kessler, Judy, 1950-   . II. Title.
    RC569.5.M8B788   1995
    616.85'236'0092--dc20   95-31824
    [B]   CIP

W.W. Norton & Company, Inc., 500 Fifth Avenue, New York, NY 10110
W.W. Norton & Company Ltd., 10 Coptic Street, London WC1A 1PU

1 2 3 4 5 6 7 8 9 0

Contents

 **Preface**

In our first book, *The Family Inside: Working with the Multiple,* I and my coauthors, Judy Kessler and Lynda Shirar, addressed the origins, symptomatology, and treatment of multiple personality disorder and dissociation. We have received many positive responses from therapists and multiples who have found this first book a helpful addition to their treatment plan and journey toward healing.

In this book, a follow-up to the first book, we address integration and post-integration as experienced by Judy Kessler. We have chosen to use the format we found so successful in *The Family Inside,* with Judy as the spokesperson for her own experiences and with me speaking from an observational point of view as a therapist.

The first chapter will cover what integration is, the changes that accompany integration, and some possible pros and cons as to its value. The second chapter will concentrate on the process of integration and the usefulness of Virginia Satir's family systems techniques in bringing about a successful ending to the process. The ensuing chapters will follow Judy closely through post-integration as she relates her own personal experiences and will be interwoven with my responses, observations, and comments.

Let me emphasize that while there are similarities between every multiple, there are also differences. Just as each child in the same family of origin differs from her or his siblings, so will each multiple differ from other multiples in the way she or he discloses past experiences. The constructs of the inner family system will reflect the individuality of each multiple and her or his own unique way of coping. Therefore, this book is neither a schematic for the treatment of every multiple nor the story of every multiple.

The intent of this book, which discusses most specifically Judy's circumstance, is to bring to the reader not only the results and the tragedy of a shattered life, or the difficulties surrounding the resurrection of a human being, but also the story of a goal achieved: integration. Though this is the story of a single individual it is a universal story for it reflects a truth that encompasses our world. Child abuse exists, it is ongoing, and it impacts us all. It is violence in its most obscene form.

The work that Judy has done to reclaim her shattered self and her willingness to share both her struggles and the outcomes has demanded that she focus on the realities of a life irrevocably altered by abuse. It is a measure of her unconquerable spirit and personal heroism that she is able to do so. It is triumph over tragedy — tragedy that never should have happened.

Judy's life has come full circle and she now faces a future filled with promise. Our hope is that therapists who are working with a multiple, whether at the beginning, in the mid-stages, or near the end, will benefit from her hard-fought and arduous journey. Judy's life, a life lived in a twilight zone not of her own making, is a true example of the incredible strength of the human spirit, yet, beyond that, she is a woman of remarkable courage. She chose not only to return to the horrors of her childhood to retrieve lost pieces of herself, but also to bravely share what she has learned with all who have suffered in like manner and those who choose to help them.

Integration, as we will show, is not an easy process; nor is post-integration the "happy ending." Yet, post-integration brings with it a life to be discovered, a life of possibilities. Every child has a right to this, and every multiple who never had a childhood deserves that same right. To every multiple who struggles, to every therapist who struggles with him or her, we wish you Godspeed.

Doris Bryant

Acknowledgments

JUDY   Many multiples have said that integration is not possible. In my experience it was and remains the most important event that changed my entire life experience. This could not have been possible without the help and commitment of my two therapists, Doris Bryant and Lynda Shirar, who were there from the beginning until the end and who remain my friends, coauthors, and colleagues.

I am grateful to Doris Bryant for her compassion and understanding, and for her knowledge of family systems combined with the skills and intuition of an artist and the humane love of a born teacher.

I am also thankful to Lynda Shirar, for being part of my therapeutic team, bringing with her the intelligence, compassion, and creativity needed to make my journey possible.

I would like to acknowledge the encouragement and support of my friends. These people cheered me on and gave me extremely helpful suggestions and insights on this project. I wish to thank Jenny Ligon, Laurie Thomsen, and Dawn Close.

I especially want to acknowledge my brother and sister, Robert and Oma Whitecloud, who have taught me to walk the red road. May the six powers bless your earth walk journeys. Pilamaya aloh (thank you very much).

Finally, I want to thank my husband, Lyndon, and my son, Donovan, whose support and love have given me the strength to continue my journey.

DORIS   I wish to thank many individuals for their continuous support and encouragement during the writing of this book.

Lynda Shirar, colleague, skilled therapist, and friend, who provided a keen eye, a listening ear, honesty, and humor throughout much of this journey.

Karen Bernstein, a treasured friend who consistently came to my rescue whenever I needed an extra hand or a good left brain.

Tricia Stewart, my fiercely loyal and loving daughter who managed my "self-care" program.

Marc Bryant, my son, for his love, steadfastness, and support in times of adversity.

Tim Stewart, my son-in-law, and Denise Bryant, my daughter-in-law, for their friendship and love.

My granddaughters, Shamarah Stewart, Talitha Stewart and Melanie Ann Bryant, my very own fan club.

Jean Decosta, Terri Trew, Darryl Herzog, and Julie Rider, colleagues and friends, for their enthusiastic affirmations.

Betty Ingels, long time friend and supporter for many years.

Sonya (Sunny) Wilt, a woman of wisdom and discernment who envisioned more for me than I could envision for myself. And finally, I would like to acknowledge and honor the one who changed a destiny of despair into one of hope; one whose life is proof of the power of life to resurrect itself; and the one who is the heartbeat of this book: Judy Kessler.

We would both like to acknowledge and thank the one who has trusted our judgment, helped in our vision, and who made this book more than a possibility: our editor, Susan Barrows Munro; and the one who guided us through the final editing, her associate editor, Regina Dahlgren Ardini.

 **Introduction**

JUDY   Creating multiple personalities was a gift I was able to use to survive an oppressive childhood filled with horrifying experiences of abuse. Yet, as an adult, having multiple personalities was agony. No longer a gift, the protective coping mechanism I had created as a child turned into a dysfunctional way of living in the world.

Consequently, I began therapy in 1985, which resulted in the unification and integration of the personalities I had created during my childhood. Even more important, integration has given me the memories, feelings, and experiences of my former personalities. It is *I* who now remembers those lost years. As a result, through the ability to recall my past, I am able to talk about my history, the history of my former personalities, and how I was able to survive. This is my story.

Each day of my existence was endured by the personalities I created to survive my childhood. They lived my childhood, my adolescence, and my early adulthood. One of my dominant personalities married and gave birth to my son. One went to church. One drove fast cars. They were young and old. Some were confident and some were frightened. Some lived an "average" life. Some lived in the fast lane. A few tried to commit suicide, while others were oblivious to my past history of child abuse. While I, the original child from whom all the other personalities were split off from, lay deep inside, asleep and dissociated, the "others" took on the roles necessary for me to live. I did not know life existed. I did not know I existed. To this day I do not remember ever "living" my life as a whole human being until after I completed integration.

The life most of my dominant personalities built for themselves during my adulthood was as "normal" as they could manage. Yet, living became difficult for them when the solid and rigid walls of amnesia built between each other began to break down. Their lives deteriorated quickly into a nightmarish existence, living each day with the feeling that they were going crazy. They heard voices and lost time. They had panic attacks and they had nightmares. Worst of all, they began to remember "the secrets."

One of my dominant personalities sought out mental health services for help, one took more drugs to drown out the voices, one went to church to be "healed," and another tried to commit suicide to end the "crazy thoughts."

What continued for years after the breakdown of the internal system were hospitalizations, one after another, for either suicide attempts or drug usage. Several therapists and mental health workers later, and with at least six different diagnoses, I was correctly diagnosed as having multiple personality disorder. After a particularly serious suicide attempt and being hospitalized for several months, Judith, one of my dominant personalities, was told she had multiple personalities. She was shocked, scared, and confused. Being the "religious" personality, she could only pray that there was a "cure." Upon leaving the hospital she was advised to continue therapy.

Judith was discharged from the hospital knowing her private hell was not over. She decided to contact the counselors at her church hoping to keep the secret, even from them, about the "crazy thoughts." She felt ashamed.

The first day after being discharged from the hospital, Judith bundled herself up with all the energy she could find and set off to see a counselor at her church. She hoped she could keep herself "together," yet she was exhausted from the effort by the time she arrived at the church office. Everything in Judith's life was so difficult now as she realized how much worse she was getting.

Judith sat down in front of the counselor at her church. Depleted and drained, tears welling up in her eyes and trickling down one at a time, she asked in a pleading voice to be considered as a new client for therapy. At the end of the hour with the counselor, Judith found she was holding onto a business card with the name of a new counselor on it. She had lost more time; thinking only a few minutes had passed, Judith wondered why she was being escorted out the door. Tired and frightened, Judith realized she was being referred to yet another counselor.

Judith desperately hoped that the appointment for the next day with the new counselor would again bring a "cure" to her "crazy thoughts" and questionable sanity. She felt hopeless and rejected.

Meeting Doris Bryant, the new therapist, was hell for Judith, yet it was the beginning of the most significant opportunity I had ever been given — the opportunity to live a normal life.

The inner personalities I had created so many years before were embarking on a journey that was to change my life forever. It was a courageous journey, not unlike one taken by any group of explorers. It was a journey into a new world, filled with adventure, excitement, and fear. It was a journey to find *me*, the original child, for whom all the other personalities had been created to protect.

DORIS   The young woman sitting so primly in my office and eyeing me with a great deal of skepticism appeared extremely anxious although she was doing her best to mask her feelings. She was immaculately dressed, articulate, and proved to be, as our conversation progressed, very bright. She began the session by challenging my expertise as a therapist, as well as my grounding in Christianity. She was looking for answers to her recent diagnosis of multiple personality disorder (MPD). She remarked that she preferred to think of herself as "crazy" rather than a multiple, that the very idea of having "separate parts" terrified her. She believed there was possibly a cure for being "crazy" through her religious belief system and expressed little faith in mental health practitioners.

Judith could not understand why her church turned her away, sending her to a therapist whose beliefs she didn't know, and therefore whom could not trust. She remarked that the voices she heard were her own thoughts, even though "crazy," and that she didn't accept that MPD was the correct diagnosis. She further explained that my role as therapist would be to help her find a way to gain control of these thoughts. This first meeting with Judith, one of Judy's dominant personalities, was merely a precursor of the years to come; years in which I was to meet and appreciate the many different personalities that held the secrets of Judy's past.

It was the summer of 1985 and MPD was still considered a rare disorder. There was little literature on the subject and even less on treatment as I was to find out. Fortunately, I'd had the opportunity to study with Virginia Satir, a great teacher and therapist, and so the treatment plan that I ultimately designed was based upon concepts I had learned from her, including her concept of "parts," as well as family systems theory, and Gestalt techniques in which I'd had prior training. I believed family systems theory would be most useful in mapping the dynamics and inner workings of what I came to call Judy's "inner family"; Satir's concept of "parts" could be expanded to "personalities"; and Gestalt techniques would address the present-day conflicts most effectively. My meeting with Judith was the beginning of an unusual opportunity to incorporate all of these concepts into one therapeutic process and with these as the basic foundation, the therapy began.

Beyond Integration

I Will Not Be Lost Forever

Lingering
asleep
between the life just past
and the still unknown
I only know enough
about myself
to know
that I don't know enough.

Nor can I say
I know what's missing
voids are voids
and only seen completely
after I've had victories over them.

By Judith, one of Judy's dominant personalities
1985

chapter 1

What Is Integration?

DORIS   "One of the major goals of treatment (of multiple personality disorder) is the reconciliation and unification of the several personalities" (Kluft, 1988). Whether the terminology is unification or integration, the end result will be the fusing or coming together of all the separated personalities, or alters, to form a whole.

It would have seemed logical, even sensible, for Judy to desire integration, to desire to become a "whole person," yet, during the first years of therapy I was not dealing with Judy, but with "dominant personalities" in Judy's inner family. The fact was, it wasn't until "reconciliation" of all personalities took place that we could even begin to work toward integration and at the time it didn't seem "sensible" to those dominant personalities who had been "out in the world" for some time and had established a life of their own.

Indeed, the very word integration created panic within Judy's inner "family system." The system that had been created for Judy's protection and survival went into chaos. While there was agreement among the personalities that the present system was becoming increasingly uncomfortable, it was at least familiar. The dominant personalities resisted the changes, which seemed to hold no promise for a future, and clung to their increasingly precarious places within the system. Their struggles will be related in more detail in the following chapter.

Before we progress further into our discussion of integration it is important to understand how and why Judy, who was born "whole," became a multiple to survive. Her story will clearly demonstrate how severe and continued traumatic abuse can cause a child to dissociate, to split over time into many different personalities, many different pieces. Her story is the story of the creation of a multiple. It is a true story.

Judy's Childhood Story

JUDY   I was born uncelebrated. I was not often held or nurtured. As a result, I lay in my crib most of the day, surrounded by the dismal iciness of gray walls. I was cold, hungry, and dirty most of the time. In addition, I was not called by a name. I was an object that was discarded and dumped in the corner of a room, only to be used and abused for the pleasure of others. I did not know I existed.

From the time I was two years old and out of the crib, until the age of five or six, I lived locked in my room, a prisoner isolated from the world outside. Only on special occasions was I taken from my room—to be used in rituals or pornographic movies.

My room was located at the top of a staircase, and I could hear if anyone approached my bedroom door. Most of the day I strained to listen for the old wooden steps that creaked and cried with the footsteps of those invading my world. In my confusion, I believed that my abusers thought I liked their intrusions; I often heard them say, "Are you ready for a little love?" Their love hurt.

My days were filled with lonely play. I craved companionship. As my need to be with people increased, I created an inside friend called "Little Judy"; she began to talk to me and I to her. I liked to hear her voice, and I could play with her whenever I wanted. I felt so glad she was my friend; she made me feel good in my upside-down world. We were inseparable. My secluded and lonely world was now filled with laughter and hope. I knew better than to tell anyone of my secret friend, for they would take her away, just as they had taken away everything else.

As the darkness of each night crept into my room, and the light of day subsided, the shadows on the wall grew more monstrous. I hated the night. Often I would cry out for help, screaming, "Do you know where I am?" It was not safe for a little girl to be alone at night in her room. I experienced the cries of other children inside my head as I sat in the corner of my room, terrified of the approaching darkness and straining to hear the footsteps of the invaders. When I heard their steps, and they reached the top of the stairs, my heart began to pump so hard I thought it would explode. Every breath was so hard; I gasped for air. I wheezed and shook as I heard the intruders unlatch my bedroom door. The doorway would then be filled with enormous, towering figures.

Unable to cope any longer with the terror of the night, the rituals filled with sexual perversions and physical pain, I created more children inside to help me. Soon there were so many, I found that I could hide safely away inside, letting those I created survive what I no longer could. I did not experience pain, for it was held by my other selves. I did not experience anger, for it was kept firmly locked inside. I only experienced isolation as I "flew" by myself above the room, watching below me as the invaders tortured the bodies of the other children I had created so that I could survive.

Years went by during which I didn't know I was human, didn't know who I was. I lived in a world of silence, shattered only by the screaming voices of other personalities. The abusers raped my body, tortured me, and took my body from me. They raped my soul and tried to take my spirit as well. They assaulted me with objects that pierced and cut and tore from me any belief I might have had that I was anything human. I was a thing, no better than a chair or a rock or dirt. I was the filth that constantly covered my body. They had taken everything from me, including my "self." Thrown around like a rag doll that had no feelings, I was given to others to be used and I was carefully instructed to give them pleasure. I thought I was rotten and evil, that this could happen only to bad little girls. I was not sure of anything in this crazy world I lived in except that I was an awful and ugly "thing" and must deserve these awful, bad things that happened to me.

I began school around the age of six or seven. School for me was like an abstract dream running in slow motion. I tried so hard to follow the rules at school. And, as instructed by the abusers, I *never* talked about the abuse or said anything about my life at home. I knew better than to tell the awful secrets. Almost daily I was sent home from elementary school for not wearing panties (they hurt), or for fighting with other kids on the playground, or for not listening in class, or for lying, or for just not being "a good girl."

I was not allowed to be involved in any outside activities other than school and I was not allowed to have any friends. My isolation continued, as did the secret abuse during the nights. From this time on the lies were well hidden behind the false facades that the abusers began to create. The abusers involved themselves in community activities such as boy scouts and attended church on Sundays. They were considered good upstanding people by others.

Life was not real. I was not real. I was only this "thing," waking each day so I could be used and abused each night. Time no longer existed for me; I hid inside, covered by layer upon layer of created personalities. I lay dormant inside myself, still and unformed. I was not a person. I had no hope, no unity, no life at all. I felt ugly and dead. I still to this day cannot comprehend how I survived, even though I know it was my ability to dissociate that brought me through.

DORIS   Judy's story, even in all its tragedy, is an excellent example of how her ability to dissociate helped her to survive the extreme and repeated abuses she continued to suffer during the first 18 years of her life. I discovered during the work we did prior to integration that she had split into over 60 different personalities. These 60 parts consisted of dominant personalities, nondominant personalities, fragments, and what I called fillers. It would prove to be no small task to gather all these parts together so they might become one collective whole.

Dissociation and the Creation of
Multiple Personality Disorder

DORIS   Dissociation is "an unconscious defense mechanism in which a group of mental activities 'splits off' from the main stream of consciousness and functions as a separate unit" (O'Regan, 1985, p. 22).

For Judy, the opportunities to pass through normal childhood developmental stages were not available. Her entire attention was focused on surviving each day, every day of her life. Her initial creation of a playmate, Little Judy, was followed by the creation of the many personalities who would live her life for her.

Although dissociation is a common defense mechanism, and one used frequently by small children, not all children subjected to even severely traumatic abuse dissociate to the extent of splitting off autonomously functioning personalities. Why do some children become multiples? (Bryant et al., 1992). Richard Kluft (1986), theorizes that four factors are necessary to the formation of multiple personalities:

First, a child must have the (inborn) capacity to dissociate to that extent. Not all people do; and because there is evidence of generational multiple personality, the ability for dissociation may be partially a familial or hereditary trait (Braun, 1985).

Second, this child who has an extensive ability to dissociate must be subjected to overwhelming and repeated trauma. In 97% of multiples, such trauma includes chronic and severe physical, emotional, and sexual abuse (Putnam, Guroff, Silberman, Barban, & Post, 1986). In some cases the trauma is nonabusive, such as a nearly fatal accident, death of a parent, etc. The definitive factor in trauma, whether abusive or nonabusive, is the presence of extreme and overwhelming anxiety in the child. The first successful use of dissociation to cope with such anxiety is followed by continued use of dissociation to cope with the subsequent hazards of life.

Third is a developmental factor, which includes the unique inborn personality and capabilities of the particular child, the time of life in which the trauma and dissociation occur, the development level of the child, and the ongoing environmental dynamics she or he lives in.

Fourth, the child who becomes a multiple is without resources that could change the situation, provide safety and support, or give the child a chance to process the trauma or abuse. In the absence of safety and support, the child is forced to use the only coping skill at her disposal.

With this information in mind, it would appear Judy fit all four criteria. Dissociation was the way she experienced continued traumatization and survived. Because there were no outside resources she could turn to for help, she created a helping system within herself that she could rely upon. For many abusive events, Judy dissociated or "split off" four separate personalities: one to hold the pain; one, the fear; one, the anger; and one, the memory. The children created during each such event remained in that particular "cluster" behind an amnestic barrier, sealed off from awareness of the other personalities and their experiences. More personalities were created to deal with other aspects of Judy's life, such as attending church or school. These became the more dominant personalities. Each of these child parts was separate from the others and each had her or his own way of perceiving and relating to the environment. The child who was sent home for fighting at school was separate and different from the child who was too terrified to speak in class, or the child who tried so hard to follow the rules. Each personality had a unique role or function. The child multiple was able to function in spite of the abuse she suffered by creating an inner "family" of parts that could perform their roles perfectly, but out of the child's conscious awareness. As Judy grew older she continued to create other personalities to meet the daily challenges in her chaotic and abusive world.

Anyone who has survived such overwhelming and chronic abuse, and who has dissociated to this extent as a result of it, will be left with the monumental task of reconnecting all the separated parts. This she must do if she is ever to recover the lost "self," the child who was born into the world whole, but who found that her only choice for survival was to give up that wholeness. Recovering and reintegrating the lost self becomes the task of therapy. For her and for her therapist, the reconnecting of these dissociated parts will mean a long-term personal commitment and years of therapy.

Terminology of Integration

Richard Kluft (1988) identified three distinguishing terms to describe the process of integration.

(1) Unification, an overall term for the personalities blending into one; (2) fusion, the point in time at which the patient

satisfies certain stringent criteria for the absence of residual MPD for three continuous months; and (3) integration, a more comprehensive process of undoing all aspects of dissociative dividedness that begins long before the first personalities come together and continues long after fusion until the last residue of dissociative defenses are more or less undone.

He (1985) further describes the more stringent criteria for integration on a group of subjects:

They all were considered to have achieved fusion, based on three stable months of (1) continuity of contemporary memory, (2) absence of overt behavioral signs of multiplicity, (3) subjective sense of unity, (4) absence of alter personalities on hypnotic re-exploration, (5) modification of transference phenomena consistent with the bringing together of personalities, and (6) clinical evidence that the unified patient's self-representation included acknowledgement of attitudes and awarenesses which were previously segregated in separate personalities.

DORIS   Using Kluft's definition, unification as well as integration is complete for Judy, as she has met all of these criteria. For Judy and for me the process of undoing "dissociative dividedness" was long and difficult, yet not without its moments of excitement. Certainly, it was always challenging. We will discuss the process in greater detail in the following chapter.

Although Kluft uses integration to mean a form of process, we use the term in the more literal sense, meaning the coming together of all parts to form a whole; this is the definition we will continue to use throughout our book.

Why Integration?

Kluft (1988) states:

Unification is considered a desirable goal by most workers in the field, although several therapists have expressed and explored the view that a negotiated settlement or reconciliation of the personalities, considered a stage in treatment by most, may be a more readily achievable and/or preferable end point or goal than unification. No controlled study has demonstrated the superiority of either outcome, but I have found that patients who achieved and retained unification fared better than those who did not. I noted that of the latter, in those patients who give priority to cooperative function, there is a spontaneous trend toward unification, while in those who give priority to the preservation of separateness, there was often decompensation in the face of intercurrent stressors, and the resurgence of conflicted clinically apparent MPD.

In addition, Dr. Frank Putnam (1989) says, "Multiples choose to remain multiples for a variety of reasons, although multiples who choose to retain their multiplicity also retain a certain amount of unresolved trauma."
Sandra J. Hocking (1992), a multiple herself, explains,

Some multiples will leave therapy because the trauma he/she is uncovering is just too painful. Leaving therapy allows the multiple to bury the trauma yet again, for a while anyway, and leaves the defense of multiplicity in place. Other multiples may choose to remain multiples because they see the loss of alters as a death and the alters themselves fear "dying." Nobody can see the advantages of being just one person when this defense has worked for years. Alters want to remain themselves. Multiples are often afraid that if they get "well," their therapist will no longer be interested in them. They are afraid that being a singleton will disrupt the relationships in their lives. They also fear the loss of their main defense mechanism, and are concerned they won't be able to handle stress and crisis without it.

While unification may be the desired goal, we believe unification is best achieved by focusing on the process rather than on the goal. By this we mean that from the beginning of therapy resolution of issues must be addressed at all levels, whether they relate to conflict between different personalities, development of new coping skills, use of nondissociative defenses, physiological and psychological changes, grief work, or learning new and more appropriate social skills. In this way all units of the personality structure will be strengthened, changes will be less threatening, and therapy can proceed toward unification, which is then more likely to be achieved.

DORIS   Dr. George Greaves has this to say about integration in his 1989 article for the journal *Dissociation*: "The therapy of MPD is transactional in nature; the therapist applies certain skills to the bipersonal process which creates the stimulus conditions under which integration takes place." There are a number of reasons why integration, or unification, might not take place and some of those reasons were very clearly stated by Sandra Hocking. However, it seems to me that Dr. Greaves provides some support for my belief that integration, total integration, or unification, would most naturally be the end result of therapy—indeed, the desired one.

There is still some disagreement among mental health practioners as to its efficacy, yet I hope this issue will be addressed as seriously as other issues in the medical community. Let me make an analogy. It is now possible for the medical community to replace poorly functioning vital organs and so save the lives and return to former vigor many of their patients. The hope is that this will not only continue, but also that improvements and simplification of the processes will arise out of continuing research in the field of medicine. It is not just a "popular belief" that the human organism functions better when it has all its parts and all are engaged in maintaining a healthy operating system; it is a known fact. Why then would we believe that it is healthy for the human psyche to perform as if a "disconnected system" were of no consequence? Would we ask anyone to continue to live at a level that is less than full functioning if we had the means to help them do otherwise? I don't believe so. In my work with Judy and other multiples, it has been my observation that while the separate personalities are of major importance for survival of the individual, they will present a challenge to any therapist who advocates change. To move them from their separateness toward connectedness requires honoring their reason for being and respecting their fears.

Regardless of the reasons for separation into many different personalities, I believe that as long as separation continues the progno-sis for a normal life, life in the fullest meaning of the term, remains nonexistent. I do not wish less for any multiple than I would wish for any other human being: a chance to enter the world with all faculties intact and operating. At the same time, I can accept that for some, just as it is for many of us, change may be too difficult, too frightening, and if that is the case I believe the most important thing I can do is to support them as they explore other options that might lead to a more comfortable and less chaotic life.

In the meantime, I salute those who continue to work to meet the challenges presented by this particular disorder through re-search and many long hours spent in committed therapist/client relationships. It is evident that their dedication and documentation of cases over the past years have added and continue to add an increasing body of information that brings hope to therapist and client alike.

To expect simplification of the process at this point in time would go beyond that which is logical, yet the very acknowledgement of the many complexities of this disorder helps to simplify the process. My hope will always be that ongoing research will support the effi-cacy of integration as the goal in the treatment of MPD.

JUDY   Not a single day goes by that I am not thankful to be integrated today and glad I made the decision to do so. The life I lead today is unquestionably different from the muddled, chaotic, and frightening life I led as a multiple. It is a transformed life. A complex life. A life filled with some rather demanding challenges and many new responsibilities; but it is a richer and more rewarding life, filled with dreams and goals I had never thought possible, never believing they would ever be possible to achieve until now.

Struggling through the hellish, brutal, oftentimes horribly painful journey toward wholeness has been far from easy. There were many times when I asked myself in despair, "Is it worth it?" But, always, the answer was, and is, "yes!"

The spirit of survival was given to me as a gift. I will forever hold deep within my heart the words of my spiritual self, "Go toward the light, so the darkness cannot engulf you." These words are a meta-phor for my life: Integration being the light—open, honest, and bright enough so I could see the truth to find my "self," while multiplicity was the darkness, which held the secrets of the horrendous abuse I suffered as a child.

I am no longer a victim of abuse, but rather a living witness to the power of the human spirit. I have chosen to confront the unspeakable human brutality, the physical and emotional anguish, and the overwhelming despair caused by the abusers. I will not give up my life to the perpetrators. I will not allow them to take from me the life I deserve to live. I will not allow them to win. In the face of it all, I have not only endured, but succeeded. This is why I integrated — to come from the darkness toward the light — and to come out whole at the end of the nightmare.

I found that hope, happiness, and health can exist even after suffering the most brutal childhood one could imagine. It took many years to get here, but I did achieve my goal. It was a matter of hanging in there long enough, and fighting hard enough. There was no way to avoid the pain — it was horrendous — but it was worth the fight to find all of me. I was worth fighting for. I have not gotten through this journey to wholeness completely unscathed, but I no longer have to suffer in shame or in silence.

Am I healed? Am I over the abuse? Have I been able to move on? In all honesty, my answer is, yes and no. I am not completely over the abuse of my childhood because the memory of it will remain in my mind and heart for as long as I live. The horrendous images these memories conjure up are more than enough to sadden and depress me on occasion. I would not be human if they did not.

On the other hand, because I chose integration as my goal, I confronted head-on the issues and problems created by the abuse. And because of integration, I no longer am plagued by the symptoms of multiplicity. It no longer threatens to destroy me, and no longer lessens the quality of my life. My history is a bad memory, a distant dream, a dark shadow I prefer not to dwell upon. Instead, I am growing, and living, and seeing the beautiful world around me. And each morning I wake to see a new day, I feel both grateful and amazed.

The nightmares are gone. The voices are gone. I no longer lose time or have a chaotic life. The haunted look is gone from my eyes. And now I am finally and truly alive. I believe that despite the horror of my experiences, I am victorious in my fight back from the pain, the fear, and the anger, to a life beyond survival. I would not have wanted anything less than full integration.

I look back now and see how terrible my life was as a multiple, how frightened and scared I was. I didn't want to stay divided, always saying, "Oh, what I could have been." No, I didn't want to be "a could have been." Instead, I wanted to give the hurt child I once was the opportunity to be filled with the richness of life and the opportunity to experience it to its fullest extent. That could not have happened if I had not integrated. It could not have happened if all my feelings, thoughts, memories, and emotions were divided, if I was not able to live and experience the wholeness of the singular knowledge of the "self."

I often wonder what my life would have been like had I not chosen integration, living instead in a cooperative yet divided way. I know in my heart of hearts there would have come a time, an experience, a "trigger," that would have thrown the inner system back into the nightmarish existence of being so frightened of life itself, but most important I would still be asleep, dissociated and laying dormant inside, unaware of the struggle. The unification process, as well as complete integration, is a unique phenomenon that I cannot compare to anything else. Yet, the incomprehensible wonder of the outcome for my life now integrated is extraordinary. The awakening of the individual true self is the paramount experience of living. It is a powerful existence.

chapter 2

The Process
of Integration

DORIS   In this chapter we will write about the actual process of integration, what I as a therapist did to encourage the process, what the process of integration was like for four of Judy's former dominant personalities and for Judy herself. We will talk about what was lost and gained in the process and what made eventual unification possible.

For the purposes of simplification we have chosen to highlight four of Judy's more dominant personalities with respect to their ages, developmental tasks, and roles within Judy's former inner family system. We believe this will give the reader a clearer picture of how Judy's dominant personalities, as well as Judy herself, were involved in the outcome.

We begin this chapter by talking about how accessing the inner family system was accomplished, how I met each of the four dominant personalities, and what their reactions were upon meeting me. We will examine their roles in the family and how meeting the core personality, the "original Judy," proved to be of major importance to the integration process. We will also discuss how the decision to integrate was made and how it affected each personality.

Therapeutic techniques used in the integration process were based upon systems theory, which made it possible to look at Judy's inside family from a systemic point of view. Seeing the different personalities as a "family" in which many "members" represented a variety of ages and stages of development also underscored the importance of each individual in relation to the system, no matter how small their role might seem. This helped me to discern more clearly not only what their needs might be but also enabled me to see them as individuals; individuals who, because of years of ongoing abuse, had very different reasons for being and very different roles to play. To view each of them as important was a matter of some significance when building self esteem and dispersing power within the system.

My use of Satir's concept of "parts" (Satir, 1978) provided the vehicle that eventually led to the unification of so many different parts, or in this case, personalities. Although there were many more personalities than the four we chose to portray in the integration process, I used the same therapeutic techniques with each one. All needed a safe place to come to do their work and all needed to have trust not only in the therapist but in the process itself. It was important to move slowly in the opening up of such a tightly closed system and establishing avenues of communication. As connections were made, awareness of one another could grow. In reframing negative behaviors as coping mechanisms designed to protect and maintain the system I was able to provide family members with a new perspective and a better understanding of one another's roles within that system. It was with these new understandings that acceptance began and there could be movement toward a common goal.

For purposes of simplification, in this chapter the terms *family, family system,* or *family member* will be used in reference to Judy's *inner family.* I will use *immediate family* when I refer to Judy's husband and son. It is because of the inner family, a family created over 35 years ago to protect the life of a little girl, that this chapter was made possible.

In addition, without denying the importance of therapy, I believe it was Judy's own strength, courage, and determination and the indomitable spirit of a "system" who refused to be denied life that eventually led to the recovery of that life—a life Judy now can truly claim as her own.

Accessing the System

DORIS   The information I had received from the hospital where Judith had been diagnosed and had spent the last three months assured me, that besides Judith, I would be meeting at least three more personalities. I was to find out over time that there were considerably more; my introduction to Judith was just the beginning. I thought at the time that she was the core personality, the one to whom all others would join when integrated, but I was wrong.

My understanding of MPD was minimal at best and I knew I would have to learn a lot more about the working dynamics of Judy's inner family before I could even begin to design an appropriate plan of therapy. Getting to know the different members and the roles they played within that system was the first order of business; getting them to accept me as a therapist with whom they could feel comfortable was the second. It would take some time.

The closed system in which the inner family operated proved to resemble that of an extremely large dysfunctional family, one that housed many secrets and much despair, one in which chaos was escalating and the energy it took to keep the family together was beginning to break down. There were many fears; a major one was a fear of "outsiders," those the system saw as intrusive or who could cause changes, like a therapist. Yet change had already begun, as the chaos indicated, and the system had begun opening up in spite of those fears.

My first task in accessing this remarkable "family" was to establish that my office was a safe place, safe enough for them to come out and just look around or safe enough for them to express themselves. If they were ever to trust me they must first learn it was safe to do so, and if we were ever able to begin the vast amount of work that lay ahead, trust was essential.

Working from the "outside" with this tightly closed system, I knew it was important for me to move slowly to gain the family's confidence. I needed to learn how their particular system operated, become aware of communication patterns, rules, and beliefs within the system, existing boundaries, and the roles each member played to keep the system intact—I could not do this if I didn't know who did what. With this information, I spent many hours getting to know as many inner family members as I could, listening to and validating each one.

By the time I realized that the inner family was much larger than I had thought, and more personalities kept coming out as the work progressed, I had accessed the system, understood the way it operated, and so was prepared to incorporate these "latecomers" into the therapy. As with any family it was also essential that I did not in any way elevate the importance of one member over the other. I honored each as playing a significant part in the system regardless of the dominance of their role. All were of value.

JUDY   I remember each personality felt "invited" to come out in therapy; this kind of remembering is difficult to explain, yet it needs explanation because at the time *I* wasn't really there. In the beginning of therapy, the child I had been initially had literally not yet been found. Since integration, I have memories like anyone else and I can recall my life experiences from childhood on. What I remember is how a particular personality managed to survive those experiences, even as I acknowledge and claim all those experiences as my own. And so, I do recall the years before integration, during therapy, and what led eventually to the unification of all my parts. This I know: The open invitation for each personality to be in therapy and the safety created in therapy for them to do so made it possible for even the most frightened to eventually appear.

DORIS   Some of the child personalities showed up shortly after Judith began coming to therapy; the older family members proved to be more cautious. The children came to play with toys and draw pictures. In fact, art proved to be a very valuable therapeutic tool for many family members. It was clear that not all of the members of this family knew of one another's existence and this is where art, along with journaling, became excellent vehicles for creating awareness of others. Pictures were a concrete way of communicating feelings and events to one another when other forms of communication were inaccessible; they were also a safe way for individual members to express fearful feelings, such as rage.

The content of some of the drawings was very clear to me; others seemed to hold meaning for the children but were meaningless to me. It was not difficult, however, to distinguish drawings of a child from those of a more mature personality, primitive figures in play dough from sculptures in clay, and child-like scrawls from philosophical writings. Even for those family members who maintained the strongest denial, it became more difficult over time for them to explain away the drawings and writings—which also offered some explanation for their periods of time loss.

Introduction to the Four
Dominant Personalities

DORIS   Judith, the first family member I had met, was a major player in the family system. She was very traditional, prided herself on keeping an immaculate house, attended church regularly, and went to bible study every week. She was also an authority on a particular breed of dog, even writing a section in a book about them.

Judith's home, church, husband, and son were her main focus. Her relationships with people outside of her own immediate family were somewhat formal and distant. She was extremely creative, although not always practical—as her choice of white sofa and chairs in a home with a small boy and two large dogs demonstrated. She attended junior college, and particularly enjoyed art classes, in which she excelled.

Always carefully dressed and very proper in her demeanor, it was very painful for Judith to live a life that was becoming increasingly "crazy." She was terrified of what she called the "evil thoughts" in her head and wished to rid herself of them through prayer, living a good life, and being a good person. Whenever Judith was faced with the reality of her diagnosis in terms of her own experiences, such as losing time and finding herself in places she would never consider going, she would retreat to the safety of religion and the promise of salvation from unremitting despair. As the despair deepened, she considered, and sometimes attempted, suicide.

Judith blamed herself for her failure to be healed, believing she was at fault for not having enough faith. Caught in a cycle from which there seemed to be no way out, she came into therapy grudgingly and only as a last resort, trusting neither therapy nor therapists, yet committed to continuing her search for release from the chaos that had become her life.

The next dominant member of Judy's inside family to appear in therapy was Little Judy. At the time I met her, I was working with a very young and very fearful child personality, when suddenly she switched and there sat Little Judy, smiling and happy to be there, although a little shy. She made many future appearances in this manner when the smaller family members and even some of the older ones became frightened.

Little Judy was always gentle, very playful, and liked to draw pictures of "pretty things." She was delighted by what she saw around her and very happy to draw "pretty pictures" for me, drawing with her left hand, as opposed to older personalities, who drew with their right hand. She was great at diverting attention away from the more serious aspects of therapy and if she felt threatened by any part of the therapy, there would be a switch and Little Judy would leave abruptly to return at a later time.

Standing in the wings, so to speak, and observing me, apparently with amusement, was Jane, another dominant family member. She did not make an immediate appearance, using her time as observer to check this therapist out. When she did appear it was with a wry grin and some discomfiture, for she had taken Judith's place in therapy and found herself attired in detested polyester instead of her favorite blue jeans and t-shirt.

Jane was the opposite of Judith, preferring a life style that had its beginnings in the "hippie" era. She was assertive, outgoing, and very knowledgeable about drugs. She was not inclined to attend church or prayer meetings, and moved in quite a different circle of friends. Keeping house was not her idea of a good time although she was fiercely protective and loving when it came to her immediate family. She also attended junior college, where her main interests were anthropology and psychology. She was to provide some lively moments in therapy.

Several months into therapy Gerri appeared. She was the only dominant personality I was to meet who loved dressing up in "pretty clothes"—no polyester or jeans for her. Her manner was one of bravado, chip-on-the-shoulder, I-don't-care attitude. Swinging one foot and gazing around my office she informed me daytime was not "her thing," she went out only at night. Gerri wanted me to know she did not do drugs or alcohol. However, her interest seemed to be directed not so much toward me but toward my cotherapist, who at the time happened to be male. She displayed a great deal of curiosity as to what his role in therapy might be and her questioning of him became rather flirtatious. I had no idea at the time what impact she was having on the other family members, as well as on the family system itself.

JUDY   Therapy for all four dominant personalities ranged from delighted to miserable. Little Judy, feeling acknowledged and somewhat appreciated did not question why she was in "the big therapy room." Instead, she felt happy and important, knowing she had someone's undivided attention. Jane, on the other hand, felt entertained by the thought that she could "play the therapy game," smugly believing she could win. In contrast, Gerri felt angry and disgusted at the idea that she was being "inconvenienced" by the questions and curiosities about her and her behaviors. And Judith felt pathetic having to admit her need to rid herself of the "evil thoughts."

Roles of the Dominant Personalities

DORIS   Although there were other personalities within the system, we have chosen the four whose roles complement one another in the most obvious ways to demonstrate Judy's inner family dynamics. For instance, each represents a particular age where important developmental issues were meant to be addressed. When Judy was not allowed to experience what would be normal for a four- or five-year-old, exploring and experiencing a world beyond her own environs, Little Judy, with her lively imagination, expanded that world by bringing inside what she knew about the outside world. Gerri obviously did her best to meet the challenge of a developmental stage that is difficult for most teenagers, understanding her own sexuality, while Jane, also a teenager, was interacting and relating to her peers. Judith was needed for that leap into maturity where responsible behaviors were important to home and family. To make these examples even more clear, following are more detailed descriptions of each dominant personality's role in the inner family and how they affected the dynamics of the system.

Judith — The Denial

DORIS   Judith quite appropriately was created when a more traditional way of life was needed. To be a mother and keeper of the home was her main focus. Very responsible and organized, she managed home, child, and husband with serious dedication. She wanted everything to be nice and pleasant and did her best to make it so. She did her best to construct a world for herself and her family in which the routine of everyday life would not be disturbed by unpleasantries. She clung tenaciously to order and structure and stood firm against change.

Judith was Judy's denial part. She wanted to believe that she had always lived a "normal" life. In fact, she continued to maintain contact with the abusers with no notion of the inner turmoil this created for those personalities who remembered the abuse and were terrified of any connection at all.

During my first meeting with Judith it was not difficult for me to see the fear beneath the mask of her self-sufficient and competent persona. Misery and despair seemed very close to the surface. Her bouts with depression had become more frequent and she had grown to distrust the medical system as a means of helping her solve her problems. She clung to the promised healing she believed would come through her faith, but even her confidence in her religion had been shaken.

I realized that if I were ever to establish an effective therapeutic relationship with Judith, I would have to create an environment in which she felt safe enough to express her fears and her misery. I did not believe this would be easy, for Judith made it quite clear she was prepared to challenge me at every point. At the same time, I believed she had reached a point of such desperation in her search for healing that she was open to new possibilities even as she fought them.

Judith was unable to correlate the chaos within herself, her depressions, and her anxieties with the fears of other dissociated parts for they remained outside her awareness, walled off by amnestic barriers; instead, she clung to her religious beliefs. Any event that occurred in therapy or outside of therapy that shook this belief meant a retreat into an attempt to be a better Christian, and I would be informed that she was seeking a new therapist. In fact, four months into therapy I received a letter informing me she was ending therapy. By this time, however, I was already working with a number of other personalities who felt safe enough to come out and continue the therapy, thus leaving Judith in the rather awkward position of finding herself in my office in spite of her obvious desire not to be there, proving the system was more powerful than the individual personalities.

JUDY   Judith resented the therapists, believing they were causing more trouble in her life than they were helping to relieve, and she hated the therapy, feeling it to be intrusive, as well as "unChristian." She felt miserable knowing she must continue therapy to "fix" her problems, while continuing to insist, "I'm getting worse, not better in therapy." Judith's confusion escalated.

At the same time, Judith was not willing to acknowledge her increasing loss of time, nor the fact that she may be a multiple. And certainly, she was NOT going to admit that the way she was had anything to do with the dreaded words *child abuse*. On the contrary, she hung onto the belief that she "had a wonderful, normal, loving childhood." "I don't know why," Judith would think, "these therapists don't believe me; it's the truth, it's always been the truth!"

Judith felt so depressed and desperate as the chaos continued to intensify and the wish for a "miraculous cure" seemed hopeless; she wished only to end the confusion and miserable life which had become hers.

Little Judy — The Distractor

DORIS   Little Judy had been created some time before the age of five. Her role in this inner family was to act as a distractor when there was too much pain or fear. Her responsibility had been to bring Judy out of her joyless, lonely world into a world where there was laughter and play. Even after Judy retreated behind amnestic barriers, Little Judy continued this role, bringing the same respite to other child personalities.

Having been Judy's only childhood playmate, Little Judy made up for Judy's deprivation when it came to companionship, real toys, or play. In her imagination she could go to the park, play on swings or catch a ball and she took Judy as a child into her imaginings, relieving for the moment the isolation and fear that marked Judy's childhood.

Within the therapeutic setting Little Judy was as curious as any child. Playful and bright, she exhibited a real zest for life, a quality that remains an integral part of Judy today. Little Judy wanted to go to the beach, dig in the sand and watch the waves, have picnics in the park, eat an ice cream cone, swing on the swings. What had been lived only in imaginings were now a reality for her and she savored every moment of her adventures. In fact, Little Judy proved to be very important, in that she already had some coconsciousness with other inner family members, particularly the younger ones.

As Little Judy became more comfortable being out in the world, she would stay for longer periods of time. She amused herself at odd hours of the day or night, playing with all the toys she found in Judith's house and leaving them wherever she had played with them, which added to Judith's increasing confusion. Even without Judith's acknowledgement Little Judy was beginning to make inroads into Judith's powerful denial system.

JUDY   Little Judy desperately wanted to please the new "big people" (therapists) in her life. She knew that she had to make "pretty pictures" for them, not wanting them to see the "bad ones." She often thought, "If I be happy, they will like us."

Little Judy often spoke in the plural, using "we" and "us," knowing the other children inside were there with her. It was up to her to make everything "okay" and help the fear the inside children felt to go away; "It's my job," she often said.

Little Judy liked being seen, liked the toys in the office, and particularly liked the "big lady." She felt safe coming to the office to play and secure knowing the "big lady" was safe as well. But it was also important to Little Judy to keep "the secrets" of the other children from being told.

Jane—The "Party Animal"

DORIS   During the high school years Jane was created and made her appearance. Rules weren't meant for her. Smoking in the school bathroom with her friends, experimenting with drugs, whatever was designated as off-limits was bound to be tested by Jane. Although good-hearted and generous with her friends, she was not the ideal student for her teachers, and her behaviors detracted from any scholastic achievements she might randomly accomplish. Her humor and sense of the outrageous livened up whatever space she occupied. She was determined to have fun and not to let restrictions set by others stand in her way. Jane appeared very abruptly in therapy one day with arms folded and a mocking grin just as if she were taking charge. She took her time surveying me as well as my office. Her body language seemed to say, "Here I am, ready to take you on."

Jane had been observing me for some time from the inside and had decided it was time to come out. I had learned from others that this ability to observe the outside world from the inside was not unusual and Jane definitely reinforced that knowledge.

Unlike Judith, who was of a very serious nature, Jane displayed a disarming sense of humor. Very much the extrovert, she had many a story to tell of her life in the sixties and took delight in "educating the therapist" about drugs. Whereas Judith had turned to religion as a means to assuage her misery, Jane had turned to drugs. It was her way of tuning out the voices she heard: voices of pain.

Neither Jane nor Judith knew the other, although Jane had some awareness of the children and eventually became very protective of them. Like Little Judy, Jane was very good at distracting, yet she was a seeker of knowledge and this was going to give her a major role in the process of integration.

JUDY   "This is a joke," Jane thought. "Therapy sucks and I won't give them a straight answer to anything if I can help it," she would snidely exclaim to herself. Nevertheless, Jane was curious, and it was her curiosity that took her further into investigating, "Why am I here in therapy anyway?" But she didn't like the answer, "MPD." On the other hand, Jane conceded, "Maybe MPD explains some of the weird noise in my head."

Although Jane had large gaps of time she couldn't remember, she assumed it was caused by her drug usage, which she certainly wasn't willing to give up, "not for nobody!" Yet, she was somewhat inquisitive about this "new thing, MPD" being the reason for it. Jane was a streetwise, wisecracking, hippie from the sixties, and surely all her training in eastern religions, gurus, and junkies would help her with the answer.

Time spent in therapy, to Jane's surprise, was actually "interestingly enjoyable." She liked the philosophical discussions on any topic she could think up to talk about, and she liked the setting, just because there was so much "neat junk" on the walls to look at. As a result, Jane decided to stay in therapy, "just to see what this MPD thing is all about."

Gerri — The Anger

DORIS   As the work continued, more personalities began to emerge, among them a teenager about 15 named Gerri. Her first appearance in therapy was brief and she spent that time charming my cotherapist, a male, yet underneath that charm I soon learned was a deep anger at males. Her involvement in therapy was rare at first; as she informed us, "I only come out at night." Going out meant she could wear pretty things and have fun. Her plan was to use men as she had been used, to pay them back, to be "the one in control," and yet this never happened. She would find herself caught in situations like the ones she had experienced from the abusers and had fought so hard to avoid.

Gerri was at that developmental stage where searching for one's own sexual identity is a normal part of growing up. She had emerged at a time when another personality could not cope with being forced to live someone else's sexual desire. Rebellious and rageful at her circumstance she fought those who continually abused her. She tried to maintain some control over her circumstances by manipulating her abusers but this only fed their fantasies. Overwhelmed by those who were bigger and stronger than she, and who maintained power and control over her body, she was fighting a losing battle.

Gerri's search now was to claim for herself that which had been taken from her: power and control over her own body and her own sexual identity. Continuing her search meant she would remain separated from the other inner family members who did not understand her behaviors and experienced them as a recapitulation of past abuse.

Although Gerri did not actively seek to create problems for other family members, her behavior took the whole inner family into frightening and abusive situations. Gerri saw herself as totally separate from the family, not comprehending that her behavior put the others at risk. The idea that all family members shared the same body was not only totally out of Gerri's awareness, but all the others' as well.

Like many who have been abused, Gerri's confusion around boundaries and feelings of powerlessness overwhelmed her determination to stay in control. Even as she fought to exert power and control over those who were symbols of pain and humiliation, the results were disastrous. For Gerri, there was neither relief nor triumph, only deepening feelings of helplessness, humiliation, and anger.

Gerri feigned indifference to the reactions of other family members, who felt she continued the system of abuse at their expense and so rejected her. Her determination to gain power and control over herself and her own body was a fight for her own honor and an important part of the system.

JUDY   Gerri loved to tease men, get them interested in her, and then dump them or use them if she could. She felt the same way about the male cotherapist. "He's cute, but I bet he's stupid just like the rest of them," Gerri thought, as she continued to flirt.

Gerri frequently felt angry at herself that she had no control over finding herself in the daytime sitting in an office with two people she barely knew. This kept happening on a regular basis and she didn't like it or the therapists. They were pushy, rude, and certainly were not going to get anything out of her if they wanted to know much about her. Gerri planned on staying in charge of the situation. "Besides" Gerri thought, "they'll just end up hating me anyway, just like I hate them, so why bother?"

As a result, Gerri felt confronted around issues the therapist had no business delving into, like, "Why do you like going out at night?" "Do you know you could get hurt?" "Did you realize this could hurt 'others' besides yourself?" Gerri argued, "What the hell business is it of yours anyway?" Besides, Gerri didn't care what they thought about her; she didn't care what other family members felt, she just wanted to have a good time. And Gerri was going to make sure they weren't going to take anything from her, including her "good times, parties, and pretty clothes." "The hell with them all!"

Moving Toward Integration

DORIS   As therapy continued and more and more members of the family decided to come out, confusion and chaos increased. Those dominant personalities who had been able to stay out long periods of time found themselves at a loss to explain where their time had gone. Amnestic barriers were beginning to break down, the closed system was beginning to open, and coconsciousness was developing within the system.

During this time, I learned that the name Judy was used as if it were the family name, but I also learned there was a Judy. Her appearances at first were brief and she seemed very shy, but as she began to feel safer she appeared more often. She was pleasant and always cheerful, seeming almost childlike in her lack of awareness, yet she appeared to be the correct chronological age and not connected to any particular abusive event or developmental stage.

This Judy lived very much in the present and didn't appear to have knowledge or memories of abuse, although she did hear voices.

She did not have any particular assigned role within the system and she was not one of the dominant personalities. She was like a shadow of what the original Judy might have been if she hadn't split and dissociated into so many different parts. I saw her as the essence of the original Judy, yet I did not know who the original might be. In fact, some of the personalities told me that the "original Judy" was dead or asleep and that they now lived out their lives in her place.

As our work continued to progress, the system continued to open even further and more of the members came out to reveal the secrets of abuse that had been hidden for years. Trust in the therapist had grown and there continued to be more coconsciousness as awareness and acceptance of the existence of others grew. Communication between therapist and personalities and between the personalities themselves was taking place as well. It was a time of serious change and there were many fears and apprehensions, which were reinforced by the introjected voices of the original abusers threatening punishment and even death if secrets were told, and yet changes continued to take place.

Support for these changes came with the appearance of Gail, a powerful and wise personality who I came to know as the spiritual guide of Judy's inner family. She knew all the personalities, was known by all the personalities, and she had been around for a long time. I now had an added resource, for Gail held a position of trust within the family and had a particularly strong connection with Jane. Gail seemed to approve of me and what I was doing, a fact that would give me even greater access to the inner family.

JUDY   Living was getting harder by the day for each personality who wanted to spend "just a little more time" in the world, and harder yet for the children who were remembering and talking about the abuse. Life for all was now terribly confusing and painful: confusing for those personalities who were beginning to hear others inside and painful for those experiencing the pain within their bodies as they told their story to not only each other, but to the therapists as well.

Jane was beginning to search for information that could help her understand her predicament; Little Judy continued to feel secure in knowing she could hide all the painful memories; and Gerri became more angry at the inner family for not being accepted as part of the group. Judith was the only one in the family now who just wouldn't cooperate, believing, "There aren't others inside."

Even more important was the emergence of a new personality, Judy, the essence. She knew she was real, but at the same time she did not feel complete. She felt as if she was floating around in time, going from one point to another, but never landing. In addition, she was confused and somewhat at a loss to explain herself, not only to the therapists, but to the inner family.

Just as significant was Jane's increased awareness of Gail, the spiritual guide. She was intrigued, amazed, and in awe of Gail, and at the same time believed they both had something in common: "a more worldly knowledge of the inner family." And it was through Gail that Jane began to explore more ways of communicating with Judith particularly, but with other inner family members as well.

Jane wrote in her journal,

I've given much thought about others inside, as to whether they are real, or whether I should continue my search for their parts within myself. Everywhere our paths cross. Like today, I met three times with several others inside, with new awareness of each. I am now aware of their slightest movement and I know this is a certain step toward recognizing them as part of me. I am becoming more aware of myself. I want to continue talking with each one, but should I recognize these parts as separate from me? Or should I claim them as myself? Our momentary meetings are not in a physical sense, and must be a spiritual one. I want to know, but I am afraid to know my many selves.

The inner family was changing. They were beginning to understand that they were each a part of something, yet understood very little about what this meant. Most were confused, some were frightened, others were inquisitive, yet all felt safer knowing Gail was with them.

DORIS   As I continued my work with family members, encouraging better and more frequent communication between them, the increasing interaction created more chaos even as it brought forth more information. The barriers between family members, once so firmly in place, were breaking down. There was more switching, both in session and out, and the more dominant members could no longer claim large blocks of time for their own, frequently finding themselves in places they would never choose to be. For instance, Judith would find herself at one of Jane's parties attired in blue jeans and a sweatshirt and Jane would find herself sitting in church wearing either a dress or something in polyester; both were horrified.

This kind of experience and others like it had made it more and more difficult for either to discount the reality of the other and Jane was the first to capitulate. She was ready to acknowledge the existence of Judith, if somewhat grudgingly. It was also during this time that Gail had chosen Jane to help connect the family and so it was Gail's influence that not only fostered Jane's acceptance of Judith, but that also led to Jane's increased awareness of the younger family members. This, in fact, was not a pleasant experience for Jane, for the sounds she once heard only faintly as background noise, sounds her use of drugs had managed to drown out, were now becoming more distinct and they sounded like the cries of children.

JUDY   To Jane's surprise she was becoming more and more attached to the inner family; as a result she was no longer able to distract or detach herself from information that was now being relinquished to her. The barriers between herself and the children seemed to have collapsed and she was flooded with pictures and information from the inner children, causing her great anxiety. Jane was horrified to hear the children — the screams of pain, the cries for help. Voices so haunting and clear, she could not use enough drugs to keep them out. She felt desperately alone, unable to help the children inside, as she began to have the children's memories of abuse. She wrote in her journal,

At times I feel so wretched with pain, I scream within myself. I must forget the past, I must rip the images out of my heart and every thought that belongs to the past shall be destroyed, only then can I be saved. And if I do not rip out every thought, even the most remote, I am lost.

Jane searched within herself for the strength needed to make the lives of each child inside better; to help them find peace; to help herself find peace.

DORIS   As Jane became a more active participant in therapy it became easier for her to see and acknowledge how her use of drugs was affecting the rest of the family. While she had a very high tolerance for drugs herself, other family members had none, or very little. This was not conducive to successful therapy since all family members lived in the same body, an idea they had yet to grasp, and the drugs remaining in the system had a particularly adverse effect on the younger and smaller children, whose work in therapy was crucial.

By this time, Jane could no longer ignore the existence of other family members. She was, in fact, developing a real fondness for Little Judy and the other children and even a rather qualified fondness for Judith. She was beginning to care, and with the caring came a certain responsibility for their welfare. To give up drugs and devote herself to the inner family took serious consideration and Jane struggled with the notion of giving up a life style that had become her refuge. It was a decision only she could make.

JUDY   Jane's appetite for drugs was beginning to slow as she realized how difficult it was for the inner children. It wasn't that she wanted to give up the drugs or the numbness they helped her feel; rather, she wanted to be more aware of the changes that were occurring inside. At the same time, she felt overwhelmed with concern for what she was beginning to discover.

As Jane became more aware of new insights, she wrote in her journal,

I am crying. Nothing can stop this dam which has given way. I'm becoming aware that I have relived childhood experiences of which I had scarcely any conscious knowledge. Until today, I had remembered only isolated fragments, but now the entire sequence is being revealed. Was this my experience? Is it possible? Was I so terribly and horribly abused? Yet, if I am a part of someone else's creation, was this their experience?

DORIS   The system had changed. Safety and trust, carefully engendered and cautiously accepted was an important factor in the opening up of this once closed system. Dominant personalities, once unaware of each other, were beginning to see themselves as a part of that system and some, like Jane and Gail, were actively participating in the change. And as the system continued to open up, the energy that had kept the outer boundary secure was no longer there. The energy that had once been available was being diffused throughout the entire system as more and more amnestic barriers fell. There was a scrambling for time and space as more and more family members came out in therapy to tell their stories, many of them children or clusters of children. Chaos ensued.

JUDY   Their lives were being lived as if in a tornado, swirling from the inside to the outside world. Rapid switching caused panic and fear. Some family members felt as if their time was being stolen by others inside, while the dominant personalities could no longer find continuity in their individual lives. Their once planned and organized lives now seemed out of control. They felt as if they were in the midst of a storm.

Remembering the Abuse

DORIS   The events that had brought individual family members such pain and suffering were now relived over and over again in therapy. This was a difficult part of the therapy. Remembering and abreacting the feelings around the event proved to be necessary before many personalities could actually integrate, and because of the pain and fear involved it was never possible for them to tell the complete story of any event in one therapy session. The story would unfold over time, but once completely told each personality seemed to know her work was finished and she could go to the "Shining Place."

It was through Jane, Little Judy, and the child personalities that I learned about the "Shining Place," a place where there was safety and comfort, a place that Gail, their spiritual guide, had taken them throughout the years when pain and suffering had become untenable or the harshness of the abuse had brought them near death. Jane described it as "a place beyond the stars where eagles fly."

The Shining Place was not only an important place of respite during therapy, but was also to become the focal point of the integration process. It was a place that was familiar to everyone, the only place in their lives that held pleasant memories, so it wasn't difficult for them to decide that the place they wanted to be after finishing their work in therapy was the Shining Place. Integration was beginning to take place.

JUDY   The inner family had changed, their energy was running out, each little child inside was now anxiously awaiting their turn to tell of their beginnings, how they were created, how they helped save the life of a little girl so badly abused, and so give up the memories and experiences, ultimately giving themselves permission to integrate, to be with Gail in the Shining Place.

The memories each child held were at first very vague, as if they were far away from the experiences they tried to reveal, so distant, in fact, that it was difficult to see the memories clearly. Even though they now believed it was safe to reveal the secrets of abuse, secrets held for many years, to tell meant reliving the fear and the pain — yet it also meant their release and the promise from Gail that they would go to the Shining Place. Trusting the therapist to help them through this difficult time, each child began to tell her individual story, not all at once, for that was too painful and scary. It was easier to release the information a little at a time, in increments, and each child did this by telling her story over and over again, adding more of the details each time, putting them in some kind of chronological order, until the fragments of information were finally put together like the pieces of a jigsaw puzzle.

Remembering the abuse was more difficult each time as each child came closer to telling her story in its entirety. The intensity of pain increased with each reliving and retelling of the experience. It was a time of reconnecting both the memories and feelings together. Having painfully relived the actual abusive incident, each child's job holding the memory was no longer needed. It was time for them to integrate.

No longer holding back the tears of pain, yet holding tight to the knowledge that their lives were now changed, the little children who told their stories said good-bye to the "big lady" (therapist) and closed their eyes to find Gail, to find a place within the inner family called the Shining Place.

Finding the Original Child

DORIS   As more and more integration continued, I noticed that Judy, the essence, was becoming more dominant. She was spending more time out, more time in therapy. She was becoming more aware and more interested in what the voices she heard were saying, and began to accept the idea that other personalities existed. As she continued to grow, to become more sure of herself, I began to hear about a child, a child who was fast asleep, a child also named Judy.

I was told by Jane and Little Judy that I would never meet the sleeping child Judy. I was told that this was the "original child," the Judy who had gone to sleep when her body and her mind could no longer tolerate the horror of the abuse she was experiencing. Judy, the sleeping child, was the reason for their being and they meant to continue to protect her.

All inner family members seemed to have a very strong attachment to this child, and even though they had grown to trust me they were not yet ready to trust me with the most valuable member of their family. This then was the core person, the one I had yet to meet, the one whose amnestic barriers were as solid as any fortress and whose importance in the integration process was unquestionable.

More personalities appeared and more integrated, while Judy, the essence, grew stronger, more dominant; she was learning more about Jane, Judith, Little Judy, and other family members. With the help of Gail and Little Judy, I eventually made contact with the "sleeping child." The contacts were brief but important for it proved to me the amnestic barriers were crumbling and that Judy, the "original child" was getting ready to connect with Judy, the essence. As

the work continued, this connection was finally made and this joining of the essence and the original child meant that JUDY was here
at last.

This new JUDY began to grow with the integration of each personality. The strength and energy she received from each one
enabled her to grow in her own strength and energy, or, as Judy
expressed it at the time, she was "becoming bigger." These personalities also relinquished their memories to Judy at the time of their
integration, giving her a sense of her own tragic history. She was
beginning to do more and more work in therapy, struggling with
new feelings and thoughts. As integration continued she grew
stronger, more powerful, but since the inner family system had just
so much energy as a whole, with energy allocated to each separate
personality, her gain proved to be the inner family system's loss. The
system's energy, while it remained the same, was being redistributed
and the energy of all remaining personalities began to lessen. For
the nondominant personalities, mostly Judy's child parts, this was
not a major problem. For them integration was desirable; it was
what they wished to do after releasing old memories and feelings.
However, the hastening of the integration process was posing problems for Judith, Little Judy, Jane, and Gerri, the dominant personalities. The loss of energy meant they could no longer stay out as long
as they once had. Having established very important roles in Judy's
life they had real fears about giving up those roles, roles that had
not only protected Judy but that had also provided them with a
life of their own, the only life they'd ever known. They became
increasingly anxious with the prospect of integration being close at
hand.

JUDY   I had awakened. I was now aware of my own existence
as a human being. Although an adult, I was keenly aware that I was
the original child, the child born into the world and from whom all
the other personalities were split off or created; created for the
purpose to survive what I no longer could. I was alive. My experience was of waking up in a world I didn't know. I thought I was still
a child. I remember looking in a mirror and seeing not the child I
thought I was but this person who had aged, was older. I was
shocked that I had aged. I didn't recognize myself, yet I knew it was
me. There was a knowledge that *it was me*; only the core person

can have that experience. The other personalities didn't have that experience of connecting with the self like the core (I) did. . . . I began to take notice of myself. I felt a shock wave go through my body when I noticed my hands; they were old. How do you describe how it feels to wake up after being asleep for 30 years? I thought I was five years old, and I was in the body of a 37-year-old woman. I thought, "My God, where have I been?" I was horrified and afraid. To recognize yourself after being gone 30 years is a shock the other personalities don't go through.

No longer did I experience myself as separate from my many personalities. Their experiences, what they thought and felt, were now my experiences, thoughts, and feelings. I was the one who had created my inner family system and filled it with many different personalities. When any one of them came out I was the one who experienced loss of time. When any of the personalities brought new information to therapy I was the one to receive that information. When memories of abuse were abreacted in therapy by any of the personalities, the memories and the feelings became mine. I was the person whose life had been shattered and who had become a multiple, and it was now my life, my wish, and my decision to become whole again. And it is I who will tell the rest of the story in this chapter, of my feelings, thoughts, and experiences during the integration process.

The Continuation of Integration

DORIS   Little Judy's work with the children was almost finished; most had integrated and she was talking about going to the Shining Place to be with them. One day in therapy, Little Judy bid me a tearful goodbye and integrated, going with Gail to the Shining Place. This left Gerri, Jane, and Judith to finish the work, yet each was having difficulty with the thought of integration.

JUDY   The sense of loss I felt with Little Judy's integration was so horrible I cried for days. I knew in my heart she was a part of me now and that I had gained back from her all that she was and had been. Yet, the feeling of loss was too overwhelming. There seemed to be an empty spot where she once lived inside. I reminisced about how I could rely on Little Judy, how she came out in therapy when I needed her, how important she was to me, and how much I wanted to tell her this. Not only did I cry, but I wrote a letter to her revealing how much I loved her and honored her existence. I thanked her for being a wonderful little girl, and told of my appreciation for all the wonderment she had brought to my life, which was now a part of me.

At the same time, as a result of Little Judy's integration, I became more aware of Jane, Judith, and Gerri. I heard their voices, I felt their pain. I felt at a loss to help them, but honored their existence as well, knowing that they too were grieving their losses, struggling to find a way to integrate.

DORIS   The next to integrate was Gerri, but before this could take place I needed to reframe her behavior in such a way that she and the others could understand the importance of the role she had undertaken—a role that was as odious to her as it was to them.

Gerri still saw herself as the "outsider" and arrogantly continued behaviors that were hurtful, leaving the others angry and frustrated. She longed for recognition and acceptance but she made it impossible. Her feelings of self-worth were nonexistent. Anger was the driving force that had taken her out into a world where she continued to battle against forces similar to the ones she loathed. It was important to her and to Jane and Judith to recognize the battle for what it was: a battle to take back power and control of her own body and her own sexuality and to wrest it away from those who would abuse it. It was a battle she had fought for all of them. That she hadn't the skills to do this was through no fault of her own; she'd had the courage to continue the fight.

I had learned that Gerri saw herself in an even more loathsome light than the others did. She could not forgive herself for her own behaviors and so held herself aloof from the others believing they could not forgive her either. It was only when she could see herself in context, as a part of a whole system determined not only to survive but to become whole, that she was able to accept the importance of her role. It was in understanding and forgiveness that she relinquished the role of reclaiming the body to Judy and integrated.

JUDY   I broke down and cried for Gerri. I finally understood Gerri and the role she had played in the inner family. I understood her pain, I acknowledged how brave she had been to fight against the abuse with her anger. I realized that in her struggle she had kept the anger for the inner family, playing it out over and over again while placing herself in situations where she tried to overcome the injustice that had once been hers alone to carry. Consequently, I found my anger.

Even more importantly, Jane and Judith realized what an integral part Gerri had been in keeping the inner family functioning. They realized how important Gerri was in protecting them, making it possible for Jane and Judith to live without the anger, and how she had been a part of their lives as well. We all mourned her loss, and at the same time gained her strength.

DORIS   Jane and Judith now had a good working relationship, and Jane obviously cared for Judith even though she still thought her stuffy. Both were now left with some important decisions. They had lived in the world for many, many years, had made lives for themselves, believed they had important places in Judy's immediate family, and had hopes and dreams for the future. The fact that they had both formed strong attachments to Judy and were concerned for her welfare added further to their confusing situation. "What will Judy do without us when she is having problems?" "Who will be there?" "Will she make it without us?" "What about our own lives?" Both Judith and Jane were apprehensive.

Jane suffered in particular; her feelings for Judy and members of the immediate family were very strong. Judith was more capable of keeping some emotional distance between herself and others, yet she too had feelings of sadness when contemplating what integration might mean.

JUDY   I felt horribly sad to find Jane's journal one day and read of her personal struggle with integration.

Sometimes I feel painfully alone, searching for the answers to integration. Alone and nowhere, I feel the pain of living and to live in pain is to live in a broken world. Everything is smashed into non-sense. Even though the storm of pain wrecks everything, the storm can clear and then renewal and rebuilding can begin. Yet, I must now be in the middle of this storm. All the questions with no answers, the yearning with no fulfillment, and the loss without any replacement leaves me on uncertain grounds. I am nowhere; no longer in the past and not yet in the future.

The Final Integration

DORIS   Integration was not a difficult concept for either Judith or Jane to grasp intellectually. They could "hear" that integration didn't mean they would be "gone," but would join with all the others, unifying and returning to Judy the wholeness of herself. It was the subjective, the notion of not being after having been, that they could not comprehend and they were fearful it would be like death. It was their love and commitment to Judy, their faith in Gail, and their trust in me that helped them make this very difficult transition. There was much grieving in the process as each made her decision to go and in saying good-bye to those they loved and must leave behind.

Jane and Judith were the last to complete a most incredible task, returning to Judy a life that had once, 38 years ago, been taken away. It was the greatest gift, and on this gift the card might have read, "To Judy, from her very remarkable 'family,' with love."

JUDY   I stood alone for the first time. Completely integrated, whole and fully aware of all those who once made up my inner family, I cried with such anguish I exhausted every bit of energy I had. Although I had gained my life back, my loss was overwhelming.

I picked up Jane's journal, and began to write.

The fact that I exist now, have existed in the past, and have a life worth living is a reality to be cherished. All of life is unique, each personality was unique and will be forever remembered. And because of you, I can not any longer reject my past, nor will I have contempt for it, as not to have contempt for each one who struggled with me to live. My life has become a work of art. The more I begin to value it, the more I will begin to value my ultimate struggle to be whole. The past has not changed but it has now assumed much greater value. And so it is with me. My past is irreplaceable. It exists uniquely, only once. It is mine. It is me.

chapter 3

Now That I'm Here, Who Am I?

DORIS   I had not anticipated that Judy would emerge from integration rather like a butterfly emerges from the cocoon—so vulnerable and fragile. She needed time to adjust to her new world. She needed to learn to depend upon her own strength and her own energy, energy that she could now claim as her own. It was not enough that Judy had found the "I" she had lost so many years ago. She had to learn to live on her own, without benefit of dissociation, without benefit of other personalities to step in at difficult times. The excitement we had anticipated upon her integration was certainly there; the celebration of the reclaimed self, a reality. It was the realization of how much work there was yet to be done that was somewhat sobering. We felt as if we were starting over from the ground up. At the same time, we knew we now had a solid foundation upon which to build a life, a life that had been shattered 38 years ago, Judy's life. The process of post-integration was about to begin.

JUDY   Working toward integration and achieving my goal to be whole was a monumental experience in my life. It meant that I

40

was no longer a multiple. Yet, being whole was more of a mystery to me than I had anticipated. What I had imagined was that after integration I would be a healthy, restored person; the person I was always meant to be. Instead, what I experienced was confusion about who I was. I needed to sort out my feelings about issues I had never dealt with before. And there were major life changes I would be making. In retrospect, I now see that I experienced and processed the outcome of integration in three stages. Each of these three stages of post-integration prepared me for my continuing journey toward healing and evolving into the individual I had worked so hard to be.

Stage 1 involved the most difficult adjustment to being whole again; adjustments to time, sound, and physical changes. Integration meant dealing with the feelings of aloneness and the continued dissociation. It also meant that for the first time I was feeling the excitement, confusion, and fear of finding myself, yet not knowing who I was.

Stage 2 was the most difficult stage of post-integration. I was working in therapy on my own, about issues relating to the abuse and, at the same time, dealing with posttraumatic stress. In addition, I was sorting out my feelings for the first time. Consequently, I was learning about what it meant to fit into the world and feel more comfortable about the new changes in my life.

Stage 3 was a time for taking charge of my life, looking toward my future and making new plans. I was able to focus on major life decisions, relationships, and to begin working on gaining my losses from lost and damaged developmental stages. It was a time of major growth.

Stage 1 of Post-Integration

JUDY   I was whole, completely integrated. The experience was a feeling of exuberance. Every voice inside became silent. I stood alone for the first time. My body felt different and strange. It seemed fuller, more expanded. It tingled with electricity. I felt taller and I could see more clearly. I looked at my hands and body as if discovering them for the first time. I was experiencing the result of integration and the uniqueness of being a person who had not been whole for over 38 years. The awareness of my new undivided self became my focus. At that very moment of discovery the question "Who am I?" roared thunderously through my head. I didn't know.

I felt scared and confused not knowing how to clarify who I was. To start the process of defining myself, I utilized the memory I had of each integrated personality. Not only had I integrated each one of their memories and experiences, I had also integrated their feelings of fear, strengths, and weaknesses. I began to perceive myself as a composite of all the personalities I had integrated. This was my new beginning.

With all the new changes, never having been a whole individual person before, I needed time to adjust to being me. It took some getting used to. Not only was I discovering who I was, I was also discovering my body for the first time and the contrast of being a singular person rather than a multiple.

Second by second I felt my life pass through the moments of time. The days seemed so long. I was living every moment of time; this was quite different than the switching and in-and-out experience I was used to as a multiple. I literally didn't know what to do with all my time. I had to learn to pace myself; at first I would start the day off frantically trying to accomplish all that I wanted to do. The problem was that I did this with such exuberance and anxiety that I was exhausted by the middle of the day. Over time, I realized the day was all mine, and I didn't have to rush through the minutes I had as if they were not going to exist in the future. And with all this time, I became exceedingly aware of not having voices.

The voices were no longer a part of me. The silence inside scared me; it gave the sounds from outside a fullness I had never experienced before. Sounds that had formerly been muffled by all the voices inside now seemed magnified. I was surprised by all the noise around me, everyday sounds, sounds I had never noticed before, sounds I had never heard: the ticking of a clock, the hum of my refrigerator, traffic in the distance, and the gurgling sounds of my coffeemaker. It took several weeks for this new orientation to be less profound.

Without the voices, I felt so alone. I was aware for the first time of the loss of my inner family, yet I viewed them as a creation of my wholeness. It was a paradox. I was experiencing the loneliness of having to be on my own, and at the same time I was beginning to understand that the integrated personalities, were actually me. Discovering the difference in how I viewed my personalities was a moment of paramount importance. I clearly realized my former personalities were parts of myself in contrast to the real people I used to experience them as.

This new learning answered my question, "Where did they go?" I was more than happy to know I had not lost anything or anyone, you might say, during integration. Consequently, I became more content, less anxious, and more determined than ever to continue my journey of wholeness.

DORIS   The fear of "losing" those parts of herself who had served her so well during the pre-integrative period was a monumental one for Judy. The intellectual concept of integration did not address the attachment or the emotional involvement the more dominant personalities had formed with Judy during their many years together, or Judy's dependence up them. During the pre-integration the younger personalities experienced some relief knowing their "work" was completed, but the older ones had invested a number of years in the system and became attached to their roles. It was difficult for them to give up what seemed to them their "lives" for an intellectualized unknown, and Judy had no way of knowing how she would function without them, what she would do without their support. Her desire to be a whole person prepared and empowered the system's ability to change.

The adjustment to her new life was both exciting and traumatic. No longer were there voices; there was now only silence. No longer did she have to conduct her life in brief and sporadic spaces of time; days and nights belonged to *her*. Decisions were made by *her*. It was during this time of adjustment that she experienced the shock of being on her own. Her days were interminably long. There were new challenges every day, new learnings, so much constant stimulation that she felt overwhelmed. And without her inner companions she felt a loneliness running like a thread through her continuing life.

JUDY   Although I was integrated I continued to use dissociation. This haunted me. I was afraid that I would not be able to maintain my integration. Although I was learning and using more cognitive skills, I couldn't seem to let go of dissociation. I had used that skill for so long that it remained a natural response for me in certain situations.

While I proceeded to use dissociation, it was different than before I was integrated. This kind of dissociation was like watching from far away; it was more like a distancing. I could peer out of myself at myself, but the difference was that I still maintained myself, the *I*. I was no longer dissociating into personalities. I had very high expectations for myself not to dissociate, yet I felt very fragile. I worried about the possibility of breaking apart again. I was afraid that I might not have the ability to stay whole. I wasn't confident in my own ability to maintain the integration that I had worked so hard to achieve.

At first I was very hard on myself: It was my fault if I dissociated or couldn't stop from dissociating. What helped me to overcome this feeling was the great amount of reassurance my therapists* gave me. They continued to tell me it was not my fault, that any type of dissociation I continued to use was perfectly natural, that because I had used it for so many years it was like using a skill I didn't even have to think about—it was instinct.

DORIS   During this beginning stage of post-integration, Judy had a very real fear of being "lost." Reassuring her that her integration was solid, and reframing her ability to dissociate as a very useful tool in her continuing work allowed her a measure of security. Her ability to put some distance between herself and the memories of terrifying events gave her a chance to continue to access information without blocking out what was essential to remember. The *I* that was Judy remained intact and no longer separated into alters or different personalities in an attempt to keep the system safe.

JUDY   The first real issue I had to sort out, after dealing with the newness of being a whole person, was my marriage. I didn't know what marriage was all about. I felt confused, as though I had been thrust into being a homemaker, wife, and mother, and was now responsible for other people's lives. I felt uncomfortable with

*Lynda Shirar was cotherapist at this time.

all of this new responsibility. I wondered how in the world I was going to handle this considering the new adjustments I was having to make for myself.

DORIS   Judy's discomfort was again the result of not having lived her own life. The man to whom she was married and the son that was born were not of her own experience, but of her former personalities. Upon her entry to the world she found herself with a ready-made family. It was as if she was required to be an adult before she had a chance to be a child or young adult and with no opportunity to select or explore a life style of her own.

JUDY   This stage encompassed an enormous amount of new discoveries: being whole and undivided, dealing with the experience of no longer having any symptoms, encountering time as different, and learning my body was my own. While I had many reasons to celebrate, I also had many reasons to be cautious.

Stage 2 of Post-Integration

JUDY   The second stage of post-integration work was difficult indeed. All the work I had done previous to integration was done while dissociated and mainly focused on surviving MPD and working toward an integrated self. Yet, with all that work behind me I still had a mountain of issues to deal with as an integrated person. The work I needed to do was just beginning.

I now focused on working through issues as a result of the abuse I had suffered. Even though each one of my integrated personalities had to deal with many of these same issues, this work was completely different because I was now working through these issues for myself, as a whole person. In addition to managing these issues, I was experiencing the effects of posttraumatic stress. That alone, prior to integration, would have caused me to dissociate, allowing other personalities to deal with the pressures of therapy, but now I was all alone and experiencing the issues myself. Feeling very vulnerable without my back-up system of personalities, I experienced this situation as if I no longer had support. I felt as though I had gained all the memories of the personalities, but not the experiences themselves. I was living as if I should know, but angry at myself that I didn't. I constantly needed to check in with my therapists, asking if I was "doing it right" as I learned to cope with everyday life on my own for the first time.

Even more important, I was beginning to discuss my thoughts, experience my feelings, and express them both without dissociation. As a result, I began working on *my* grief, *my* losses, *my* issues of separation from my abusers, *my* feelings of guilt and shame, and expressing *my* rage. At the same time, I was beginning to realize my disappointments, joys, and challenges as a result of integration. I was overwhelmed at the prospect of so much more work ahead.

DORIS   At this point Judy was beginning to pull together the learnings she had retained from her integrated personalities and was adding to them from her own learnings and experiences. It was not an ideal situation. The skills acquired from her past were reactive and survival-oriented and did not always lend themselves to present-day events. The past continued to intrude on the present in ways that did not allow Judy the security and flexibility she needed to explore new avenues. She was constantly on guard and frequently discouraged at her inability to know what she had never been taught. She blamed herself for not knowing. When Judy was able to acknowledge the extent of damage done by the loss of so many developmental stages, she was relieved in some measure of the shame and self-blame she had taken upon herself. She was able to see more clearly the work that needed to be done and understood the enormity of the task.

JUDY   By this time I was looking honestly at the person that I was. I was fully aware of my life as a multiple, that is, before I was integrated, including the suicide attempts, the self-abuse, the hospitalizations, the confusion, the therapy, the pain. I was beginning to acknowledge that this too was part of who I was, part of my history, part of my life. I was so angry.

I was also now aware of how terribly abused I had been. I now understood completely why I had become a multiple. This knowledge penetrated the depths of my soul; I was flooded with tears, feelings of anger, shame, guilt, and the unanswerable question, "Why?"

I felt as though my life was beginning at age 38 and that I had lost so much. I felt overwhelmed by the losses: my childhood, my teenage years, my young adulthood, my innocence. This was the first time *I* had experienced the losses, and a depression I had never felt before engulfed me. I surrendered to my own feelings, knowing for the first time I was mourning for myself. Finally, I was able to feel and express what I should have been allowed to express as a child.

DORIS   Stage 2 of Judy's integration was marked by bouts of depression and grief as she struggled with her many losses. As she began to realize and accept the extent of her abuse and feelings of anger began to emerge, she also experienced great anxiety. She had no way of expressing what she had repressed for so many years and the intensity of feelings was at times overwhelming. Now, not only were there the challenges of everyday life to be met, but also a roller coaster of emotions. Integration along with new awarenesses and feelings became a very mixed blessing indeed.

JUDY   Stage 2 was a difficult journey on my own. I was learning more about who I was and how to live in the world as a whole person. Consequently I was now dealing with the issues of the abuse which caused me to become a multiple. While I continued to use some dissociation, it was becoming less frequent. The intensity of feelings I had for the first time seemed insurmountable at times; and on the other hand I felt as though I would find, after all the hard work, a peace within myself I had never known before.

Stage 3 of Post-Integration

JUDY   By stage 3, I had begun to settle down into my new life. I felt an enormous sense of relief and a great measure of strength which came from knowing that I was in charge of my own life. I knew that I had choices. I had a good understanding of my past, and what I had been through. I had done a great deal of work over my many losses, and yet realized there was much to do. I began to look at what I could do with my life and my future. I was beginning to feel good about me, about new beginnings, and for the first time I began to realize my dream. I was beginning to live my life, not just survive my past.

Being in charge of my own life was an enormous change, as well as a challenge. I felt empowered, yet, paradoxically, I also felt exposed. Prior to integration, my personalities were afraid they would ultimately die because of integration; they believed they would no longer exist, or be able to fulfill their life dreams or be a part of living. I also feared they would die during integration. I believed I would no longer have access to the only "people" I ever trusted, the only "people" I thought could protect me. On the contrary, what my experience was, and what I found to be true after integration, was I had lost nothing, no one had "died," and I was not alone. My fears of loss were replaced by an experience of having gained access to myself. In other words, without dissociation, I was able to access different parts that were once my many personalities. I found I could choose to act or think in ways that were at one time attributed to particular personalities. I had so many options to choose from now. What was once separated from me was now my own; the integrated knowledge and strengths I had available I was now able to use in an advantageous way.

Even more important is that prior to integration I did not believe I had my *own* strength to survive; I relied on dissociating to the separate personalities and their strength. I now realized that strength was still available to me; it was mine, it wasn't separate. It became my own strength to survive.

Although the fears of my past continued to be intrusive, they were no longer as intense, and I found I was capable of handling them. I could move beyond the fear, which at one time immobilized me, and recognize and utilize the strengths that were inside myself. This continues to be an empowering experience. I felt as though I was able to cope with almost any situation. Knowing I could access that strength within myself, I began to tap into an energy I had never before known as my own.

Just as significant was the fear and belief that each personality would blend together to make one person and that I would lose the individual aspects of each personality. This was not my experience at all. What remained after integration were the individual characteristics of each personality. It wasn't a mixture or blending together of them to make *me*; on the contrary, they *were* me and I now had free access to every part. I gained a greater knowledge and had more available to me than I had as a multiple. As a result, I became fully aware of why I acted the way I acted, where my feelings came from, and I could more easily accept my own behaviors, thoughts, and feelings. Integration has given me the experience of being fully human; living a full life. I can now be the owner of who I am and who I was meant to be.

DORIS   Stage 3 meant that all the pieces of the puzzle that had made up Judy's life had come together. Questions she had prior to integration were answered, the main ones being, "What will happen to all those parts of me, those personalities I have known as separate beings, when I integrate?" "Who can I trust to be there for me when I'm on my own?" "Will I survive?"

Although the initial experience of integration brought with it a sense of loss and uncertainty, the ultimate experience was one of empowerment and wholeness. Rather than losing those parts that had been separated, Judy found they had indeed joined with her to become resources of strength and information to be accessed at will. As a result, she became aware of what the diversity of those parts brought to her singular life experience. The excitement of knowing that her life was no longer just a matter of survival, but one of hope, one with a future, and that she could now implement every part of herself in that future was a reality she had never dreamed possible.

Intrusive memories remain a part of Judy's life. The losses must still be acknowledged and feelings about those losses owned. Yet, her coping skills continue to improve and her forward motion is no longer impeded by the lack of knowing where these feelings come from. The remembering and the pain and sadness that come with that remembering are now hers. So is the strength.

JUDY   In this stage, I was also aware of how differently I was participating with my spiritual self, the wise and powerful presence who had literally kept me alive all these years by sustaining me with her strength and wisdom. As a child I had known Gail, my spiritual

personality, as my only resource of nurturing, caring, and uncondi-
tional love. She was there for me during the many terrifying times
of my childhood when, because of the severity of my abuse, I believed I was near death or believed I was dead. During integration
Gail was both guide and comforter for the many personalities who
made my unification possible. Following unification I knew she too
had integrated—had become a part of every component of myself.
Gail was no longer separate from me, as if she were a separate
personality, nor was she needed any longer strictly for survival; she
now permeated everything I was. However wonderful this was, I
nevertheless had a sense of loss; I was no longer able to call upon
my spiritual personality like I had over the years. What was once
available to me is no longer available to me in the same way.

As a child, I created a place inside myself called the Shining Place,
"a place beyond the stars where eagles fly." This special place was
were I felt protected, loved, and cared for. It was where I experienced everything I couldn't get in my abusive world outside. The
Shining Place was the gateway through which love could enter into
my life. In addition, I created Gail, my spiritual personality, who
could provide for me the nurturing I was being so deprived of. She
gave me understanding, warmth, respect, peace, and the feeling of
being held and comforted. And in the Shining Place I could believe
in my own goodness and that I was loveable. This replaced the
deep-felt injuries and the horrible feelings of unworthiness. My creation of the Shining Place and my spiritual personality was how I
survived what was by any other words unsurvivable. It was this part
inside, the life spirit, that led me through the abuse and through the
healing process; it was this voice that I trusted.

I can no longer escape into the Shining Place. When I experience
pain I can no longer rely on my spiritual part to comfort me. There
is still a longing to have what I once had. Consequently, I found I
still needed the nurturing, the caring, and the acceptance, and I can
now reach outside myself to get these needs met with safe and
supportive people. I also reach within myself to meet that same
need—I can nurture, care for, and accept myself.

The gift that remains from my experience as a child is the belief
that I do deserve all the things my child parts experienced while
being in the Shining Place. I can now see myself as my spiritual part

saw me, an injured child—innocent, pure, and loveable—and now I can embrace her.

I've begun to tap into my spiritual self again, which has become an enabler, giving me power, helping me grow, helping me heal. This knowledge has become more solid and more grounded; and although I now experience my spiritual self very differently than I did in the past, it is no less powerful.

DORIS   Prior to integration the spiritual personality had played a very important role. According to all the other personalities, it was this part who had created the Shining Place, an inner safety zone and resting place, as a relief from the intense abuse. I have no idea how such a wise, nurturing, accepting, and loving personality came to be. I know that Judy did have a very brief encounter with one loving individual in her early childhood years, but it is difficult to believe that it could have enabled her to build those few acts of kindness into a powerful creative personality. The wisdom and support of this particular personality went far beyond what any child could have known. In the early days of therapy and throughout the integrative process I found the spiritual part to be a source of information as well as a reliable guide in matters of the therapeutic process. This was one of the more remarkable aspects of my work with Judy, one that I still hold in awe, and is for me a powerful reminder that we are more than the sum of our parts.

When integration was completed, Judy was no longer able to access that part of her in times of stress and felt the loss of her inner nurturer deeply. Yet, the spiritual strength that supported her through the years remains and is very much in evidence as she continues her post-integrative work of expanding and directing a life that is now her own.

JUDY   As I worked through these different changes in stage 3, I also began to realize my own potential. I began making decisions that would effect my future, something I'd never done before: decisions about education, career, and what interested me. I was beginning to take new risks and explore the world around me. I was growing. I had awakened.

It was a time to use the talents within myself, a time to explore and sort through all the different interesting and exciting things I saw around me. I could choose to develop those areas of interest that brought meaning into my life. I began to enjoy what I had, to celebrate life.

The encounter with my true "self" had begun. It was at times overwhelming and yet as I worked through the issues of stage 3, the feelings of being a person worth celebrating, of being a valuable person, flooded me. There was a sense of self-caring I had never known before. It was as if I had entered another whole new world in which everything looked and felt so different. There was a quality of joy, spontaneity, and enthusiasm to my life I had not experienced before.

The search for my missing self was over. The time had come to reclaim that which should have been celebrated many years ago. The time had come to recognize my talents and utilize them in ways of my own choosing, and to access my spiritual self in a new way. The time had come to build a solid foundation out of the damaged remains of a childhood whose losses included the developmental stages necessary for a healthy life.

DORIS   Post-integration was not what Judy or I had antici-pated. The extensive individual and group work I had done with the inner family members was but a prelude to the work that was to follow as Judy began her own individual work. Pre-integration had been a gathering together of all of Judy's resources, resources that had been separated to assume separate identities and yet shared only one energy source. In this sharing, the energy was spread throughout the system with the dominant personalities receiving the most. The integration, or joining, of all the personalities allowed Judy to reclaim this energy as a singular person and to focus this energy on her post-integrative work. There was much work to be done. The many losses Judy had experienced and the nature of those losses did not leave her well-equipped to cope immediately with the new life she was experiencing. There were adjustments to be made as she realized the scope of those losses, and with the advent of being "her own person" feelings she had never experi-enced needed to be sorted through. The three stages of post-integration were to play an important role in the way Judy was able to process information as she continued her therapy.

The intense desire to overcome, to live (always a major element in Judy's life), remains a strong motivator. Having a life she can now claim as her own has brought her great excitement and joy, and her spiritual strength continues to give her the courage to work through the most difficult situations.

chapter 4

Lost Developmental Stages

DORIS   In my work with Judy, I know that her childhood needs were rarely, if ever, met. Splitting, dissociation, and the creation of personalities compounded the development of the very stages that were to prepare her for life as an adult. They were not only missed, but when the *I* or the core child got lost in the struggle to survive, life experiences were lived by other personalities. The skills acquired by these personalities were strictly survival and adaptive skills and not conducive to the healthy development of a "whole" child. The loss of 18 developmentally important years continues to have a major impact on Judy's life, even after integration. In this chapter we will present the problems that this has created for Judy in the present, and try to project what it may mean in her future.

Stage 1: Birth to 1 Year

DORIS   The first year of life has a fundamental impact on a child's development. It is during this time that the child's foundation

54

for the remaining developmental stages is set (see Table 4.1). During this developmental stage a child needs to feel that the environment is safe and that she can trust her caretakers to meet both her physical and emotional needs. These needs are basic to humankind for we are all born into a world where, as children, we are powerless to control either our environment or our caretakers.

In this stage of total dependency a child learns about who she is and what the world is like from her primary caretakers who are, usually, her parents and other family members. When there is healthy parenting, an infant's view of herself and the world is a positive one; when the parenting is dysfunctional, the outcomes are quite different.

In Judy's case, abuse and neglect were severe and began during this very early stage. Rather than learning she was a valuable being in her own right, neglect taught her that her needs, and therefore herself, were unimportant. Abuse taught her that the world was not a safe place and there was no one to care for or protect her. She learned that closeness meant pain and separateness meant neglect. She learned that her body did not belong to her. Personal space and personal boundaries were nonexistent. There was no one she could trust.

JUDY   After integration, I became exceedingly aware of how the loss of the first developmental stage effected me. I am learning about personal space and boundaries, and continually struggle with feelings of safety and trust in my environment and in relationships. Consequently, this has effected my intimate relationships, my personal relationships, and environmental relationships.

I feel emotional and physical safety in my intimate relationships within my family, which includes my husband and son. I have trusted both throughout my therapy, and my continuing healing process. My healthy relationship with my family is something dependable to anchor to, a foundation to build on, which allows me to work on safety issues outside the family. Without this safety in my home, I would not be able to explore and grow in other areas as I'm doing now.

As a parent, I am also learning about boundaries. Saying "no" is difficult for me. I am learning what is appropriate in raising a child by using my intellect and gathering information from other parents and books on the subject. As I watch my son's own development

TABLE 4.1
Stage 1 (Birth–1 Year) of Normal Child Development and Development of MPD

Psychosocial Tasks	Healthy Parenting	Dysfunctional Parenting	Outcomes of Abuse for Child	MPD Development	Outcomes for MPD Adults
Trust in environment and caretakers Being taken care of	Meets infant's basic needs; allows infant to discover body boundaries. *Messages* "You're human." "You're important." Your needs are OK."	Neglect Abuse Objectification *Messages* "You exist only when I want you." "You don't have needs."	Mistrust Anxiety *Messages to self* "I'm not important." "My world is not safe."	Need for dissociation Infant may split off newly forming personality parts: wants, needs, feelings	"I don't know where I end and you begin." "I can't trust any one." "I have to take care of *myself*."

Columns 1–3 based on Erikson, 1950, and Clarke, 1978; columns 4–6 from Bryant et al., 1992, p. 46.

through the different stages, it has helped me to learn more about myself and what it is I must learn to regain what was lost in my life.

Personal relationships outside my immediate family are habitually more difficult. I don't instinctively perceive personal relationships as positive. Instead, I am apprehensive that this kind of contact may be a negative event and I approach it with great caution. In addition, I still use old coping skills to help me explore the issues of trust in personal relationships: I read between the lines, I read body language, and I listen for the tone of voice. Safety and trust means learning to believe what someone says: I continue to protect myself, checking out safety and trust in my personal relationships.

Indeed, I work hard at believing there is trust; that I can trust at least some people. I find I am still influenced by the old message, "You are not important," and I fight to experience my own importance in relationships. I also struggle to accept that "I am loveable" and "good enough" to be in a relationship, and I often project these struggles onto the people with whom I am having a relationship. This makes healthy relationships extremely difficult to maintain.

Just as significant is my difficulty with personal space and boundaries in relationships. Having personal boundaries of my own and recognizing them in others is constantly confusing—it seems almost a foreign concept.

As a child, I experienced both neglect and invasiveness; I learned my needs were not important and that I had no boundaries. I had to draw on my own inner resources to meet many of those needs. Consequently, I don't expect my needs to be met often in relationships with others. Yet, at the same time, I have a strong desire to have them met. It is a double bind I constantly feel. If I express my own needs I feel guilty. On the other hand, if I do find someone who will meet those needs, I don't know how much to ask for, I don't know how much is too much. It gets really mixed up and is a continuing struggle.

As a result, interacting in personal relationships outside my family is exhausting. I put so much energy into protecting myself and reacting, rather than interacting. I'm constantly attentive to how I'm interacting with others and thus can't relax and enjoy myself. I'm always watching to see if I'm "doing it right." I stay very guarded.

Furthermore, I don't often initiate new relationships; when I do, it is a difficult, sometimes strenuous attempt. This has kept me from creating new relationships with new and interesting people, experiences that would be enriching.

Isolation, a painful legacy of my childhood, is one of the ways I continue to protect myself. I maintain very rigid boundaries with the outside world, as did my abusers, where boundaries kept the outside world out. Though now self-imposed, I continue to repeat the pattern in the present, having lost the first developmental stage of trust, safety, personal space, and boundaries.

DORIS   Judy has created within her own family, with her husband and son, a closed system similar to her abusers', but there is a major difference in intent. Whereas her abusers maintained a closed system to keep pernicious secrets and perpetuate abuse, Judy has constructed a closed system that is loving, accepting, and protective. It is within this system that opportunities for new learnings about safety, personal space, and boundaries become available to her. This has provided her with a base from which to work and therapy has allowed her to expand that base. To extend herself outside of this construct she must continually confront her feelings of powerlessness in interpersonal relationships. Control issues arise as new experiences within these interactions involving personal space and boundary issues are addressed. The need for safety becomes more intense. Feelings overwhelm cognitive skills. At this point Judy is not only dealing with the loss of the first developmental stage, but other developmental losses now add to the intensity of the situation. When feelings of inadequacy begin to emerge, Judy returns to the one place where she feels accepted, acceptable, and safe: her home.

Stage 2: Age 1 to 3 Years

DORIS   In Judy's young life, her abusers were closed and enmeshed in the extreme; there was no such thing as autonomy. Each member seemed joined together, almost in a physical sense. Judy learned at this developmental stage that her normal needs for autonomy or personal control would not be met (see Table 4.2). Her environment was not one of enrichment, but one of impoverish-

TABLE 4.2
Stage 2 (Age 1–3) of Normal Child Development and Development of MPD

Psychosocial Tasks	Healthy Parenting	Dysfunctional Parenting	Outcomes of Abuse for Child	MPD Development	Outcomes for MPD Adults
Autonomy Personal control of body Doing things "on your own"	Allows child to separate *Messages* "I am me; you are you." "You can have some control." "It's OK to do things." "You can think and feel."	Separateness is punished Engulfment or abandonment *Messages* "I control you." "Control yourself." "You're doing it wrong." "Be the way I want." "Don't think, don't feel."	Shame and doubt Helplessness Anxiety Overcompliance vs. hyperactivity *Messages to self* "I can't do it/I have to." "I feel out of control." "I am bad." "I won't feel."	Dissociation allows splitting off good vs. bad behavior and containment of "bad" feelings	"I don't know what to think or feel." "I must always watch and see how others do things." "Wants and needs make me feel out of control." "I must be in control."

Columns 1–3 based on Erikson, 1950, and Clarke, 1978; columns 4–6 from Bryant et al., 1992, p. 46.

ment. Doing things on her own was not only discouraged, but literally out of the question. Any needs she had, or expressed, were considered "bad" and punishable—unless they fit in with the abusers' needs. So she herself labeled them as "bad" splitting even more in her attempts to adapt herself to the needs of her abusers in order to physically survive.

Judy learned to "read" the people around her by watching body language and facial expressions, listening to tones of voice. She learned to deny her own needs. She learned she was not the "owner" of her own body, that it was merely an object to be used and abused and abandoned at the whim of her abusers. Pain and humiliation at the hands of her abusers increased.

Dependent upon her abusers for survival, she developed a deep fear of abandonment. Losses from her first developmental stage were reinforced. She could trust neither her environment nor her caretakers. In order to be "taken care of" she must learn to comply. Autonomy, discovering a sense of self, was out of the question. Separation from the abusers was impossible.

JUDY   I continue to encounter confusion between autonomy, being on my own, and feelings of abandonment. Sometimes I don't know where I begin and other people leave off. I often feel enmeshed to the extreme. Indeed, separateness and autonomy are difficult for me; concepts I am just now learning. In fact, I sometimes experience them as abandonment and feel neglected. Since I never experienced autonomy in others, I get confused when I see others being autonomous.

Consequently, the turmoil caused by my feelings of abandonment are painful. For example, if I feel separated or abandoned, I ask myself, "Am I bad?" The old message "I feel bad, therefore, I must be bad and deserve to be abandoned" begins to take over. Then I begin to confirm the old message, convincing myself that I am not lovable, not good enough, and always bad. In other words, I can cognitively accept if someone needs to disengage from me; I know it in my head, but not with my feelings—I feel trashed and really confused.

At the same time, personal control in relationships is a major issue for me in feeling safe. I frequently experience the need to control my environment. When I don't have control, I feel out of control, and as a result I become very frightened, wondering, "What will happen next?"

Because I never experienced autonomy in my childhood, issues of trust, fear of abandonment, and loss of control are still feelings I experience. Unfortunately, integration and post-integration work has not automatically solved these problems caused by the loss of this developmental stage.

DORIS   The loss of developmental stage 2, where autonomy and separateness are initiated, creates major problems for Judy in interpersonal relationships. While the closed system of her present family unit provides safety for individual members, it remains exclusive. Inclusiveness is peripheral with those persons outside the family and the few who access must literally "join." If they do not they are suspect. Even as Judy's cognitive awareness of the family dynamics expands, the feelings of insecurity that accompany changes in environment or relationships remain. Autonomy in others is experienced as a form of rejection, autonomy within herself is experienced as a form of isolation. Separateness means loss of contact and fear of the unknown; an unknown over which she has no control and which carries within it negative implications either at a personal or environmental level.

Stage 3: Age 3 to 6 Years

DORIS   It is in developmental stage 3 that a child's confidence in her own abilities evolves. She learns to separate the real from the unreal as she explores her world, checking her perceptions of reality against those of a trusted guide. She learns more about her own personal boundaries and the boundaries of others. These learnings are implemented into her daily life and she is encouraged to pursue them further in age-appropriate situations (see Table 4.3).

As she explores this expanded and expanding world, taking risks, the knowledge that others will be available to her if and when she needs them gives her the security she needs to continue to risk. She is able to test her own power, to learn about what she can control

TABLE 4.3
Stage 3 (Age 3–6) of Normal Child Development and Development of MPD

Psychosocial Tasks	Healthy Parenting	Dysfunctional Parenting	Outcomes of Abuse for Child	MPD Development	Outcomes for MPD Adults
Taking initiative Taking risks Exploring Separating real from not real	Provides safety for exploration; defines real vs. not real *Messages* "I will protect you." "You can do it." "You don't make bad things happen." "You can still have needs." "I will be here when you need me."	Constriction and/or neglect Confusion Double bind messages *Messages* "If you risk/initiate, you'll get hurt." "If you get hurt or if I get hurt, it's your fault." "Don't trust yourself." "No one will protect you."	Guilt Anxiety Entrapment Role reversal Hypervigilance *Messages to self* "I'm to blame." "I'm responsible for making others feel good." "It's my fault when I (or others) feel bad."	Increased use of fantasy and dissociation Splitting of reality, moral values Dissociation of personality states allows accommodation to double binds	"If anything goes wrong it's my fault, and I must punish myself." "I still don't know what is good, bad, real, or true." "I can't trust myself."

Columns 1–3 based on Erikson, 1950, and Clarke, 1978; columns 4–6 from Bryant et al., 1992, p. 47.

and what is out of her control. She can rely on "protectors" to be there for her if her explorations take her too far afield, to set safe boundaries for her, and to give consistent support. This kind of security creates a safety zone from which she can access the larger world, developing her newly learned skills as she continues to initiate and take risks.

JUDY   I am currently developing skills for going out into the world, exploring, initiating, taking risks, and making decisions on my own. As I develop these new skills, I must still contend with an old feeling: fear of change. In fact, risk taking clashes head-on with the old message, "Change means something awful is going to happen." I am not very flexible when it comes to any kind of change; as a result, I am always vigilant, moving slowly, and designing new strategies so I can take new risks. For example, I ask myself, "What will this change mean to me?" "Will I be safe?" I have found venturing out and exploring relationships is considerably more difficult than taking risks and exploring the world.

I often think I am responsible for all outcomes in relationships. This, of course, is absurd thinking. Yet, it comes from believing as a child, "I am responsible for what happens." This sense of responsibility and self-blame certainly makes exploring relationships more difficult. In addition, I question my own experience and observations in relationships, not believing that what I hear and experience really are what I hear and experience. I don't trust myself, which makes distinguishing real from unreal difficult.

The damage of losing developmental stage 3 is the remaining conflict of moving toward initiative and risk while learning to experience change as positive. At the same time, the most difficult loss I am working hard to retrieve is believing in and acknowledging my own perceptions of myself and the world around me. It is this loss which can make my world seem distorted.

DORIS   The loss of developmental stage 3 is significant for Judy. Losses in the first two stages were compounded in the third. If a child is going to explore and take risks, to use her own initiative, and learn to distinguish the real from the unreal, she must be provided with the kind of safety that allows her to do just that. Judy had already learned she had no protectors and that the environment was hostile to any kind of exploration she might attempt on her own. Her life had been one of confinement since the beginning; first it was the crib, then the bedroom. Any changes in routine, any "outings" only meant more pain and humiliation. Any toys provided were used only as props to set up further humiliations. What was "bad" and what was "good" became even more confusing to her. Double binds and double messages were constant; separating the real from the unreal was not possible when her own feelings about what was bad were discounted and called good, when behaviors that pleased others shamed her.

Exploring the world in ways that were not possible for her in the past has become a priority for Judy. As long as the initiative is her own and the risks she takes are within her control, her safety is not threatened. It is when changes occur within her environment over which she has no control that she experiences anxiety and confusion. She has few internalized resources to draw from in the realm of healthy relationships. She is overwhelmed by what she thinks others expect from her, what she expects from herself, and what she expects from others. It is during these times that Judy returns to her "safe place," her present family unit. There she can regroup and prepare herself to enter the world again.

Stage 4: Age 6 to 12 Years (Latency)

DORIS   Stage 4 is where a child becomes increasingly involved in the world outside her home, a world for which healthy transitions through prior developmental stages have prepared her (see Table 4.4). Judy was not prepared for this world. Her only social interaction at this point had been restricted to the closed system of her abusers and their circle of friends. The focus of this social group was to continue the abuse while maintaining absolute secrecy. It was, therefore, very important for them to continue to maintain absolute control over Judy's life away from home, just as they did at home. The closed system prepared for this event by becoming even more

TABLE 4.4
Stage 4 (Age 6–12) of Normal Child Development and Development of MPD

Psychosocial Tasks	Healthy Parenting	Dysfunctional Parenting	Outcomes of Abuse for Child	MPD Development	Outcomes for MPD Adults
Competence Intellectual and social skills Experimenting with ways of doing things	Allows further separation, with boundaries and support *Messages* "You can trust others." "The world is an interesting place." "You can use thinking and feeling to help you know."	Isolation *Messages* "Don't tell our secrets." "The outside world will hurt you." "Home is the only safe place."	Inferiority Anxiety *Messages to self* "I can't think/act for myself." "I'm stupid/wrong." "If I fail it's my fault." "I'm a bad person." "I must try to look right."	Advanced dissociation allows encapsulation and disownment of abuse "Created selves" perform as needed in outside world Intellectualization, denial, and copying increase as ways of coping Dominant personalities may begin to form	"I have to conceal how or who I really am." "I must keep the secrets." "Nothing bad happened." "I must look OK."

Columns 1–3 based on Erikson, 1950, and Clarke, 1978; columns 4–6 from Bryant et al., 1992, p. 47.

tightly closed. Separation from them in any way was discouraged. Evidence of any movement in that direction was punishable. The abusers Judy could not trust also taught her the world outside could not be trusted. The abusers were the only world she had known, and even though it was a hurtful and sometimes terrifying world, her captors portrayed the world outside to be even more terrible. The familiar was less fearful than the unknown, the secrets must be kept. Appearances of "normalcy" became even more important to the abusers at this time.

Judy could not in any way experiment with new ways of doing things, develop her own intellectual and social skills, or acquire the competence that would build good self-esteem. She no longer had a self. By this time, in the words of other personalities, "Judy had gone to sleep." New personalities were created to make it possible for her to live in her two separate worlds — the world of the abusers, and the world of school. Rather than experiment on her own in this new environment she watched and copied others so she could do it "right." By denying what happened with the abusers, she could have a life outside. This meant advanced dissociation in order to disown the abuse. This also meant more "switching" as her own inner system began to develop. Because this system was created by the formation of new personalities whose behaviors were copied from observation of others or what she had constructed from previous and erroneous learnings, it was frequently off-balance. Her energies were now directed three ways: toward her inner world, toward home, and toward school. There were pressures on all three fronts. Concentration was impossible. Intellectual and social skills were learned by rote, watching and copying her peers, who were not always the best role models.

JUDY   I realize now that there were at least two decades of history I had missed by not going to school, by not really being there, by having personalities live my life. Even though my personalities, after integration, left me with their knowledge and what they had learned socially, it was not my *experience*. As a result I feel inadequate and lack confidence in these areas. I think sometimes I will never be able to completely catch up. I have to work extremely hard to develop my social skills. At present, I use my cognitive skills, watching others and how they behave in social settings. I watch and copy their behavior. In fact, this is how I live in the world. I stay hypervigilant, always watching and learning how to "do it right." It is the same way I used to live as a child: to be what others wanted me to be. Now, I learn what others see as "normal" and mimic their behavior. This is because I feel so awkward and uneasy in social settings; I don't always know the appropriate behavior that fits a particular situation. I dread making a mistake and then feeling embarrassed. I become apprehensive and my anxiety begins to build. I ask myself, "How am I going to handle this situation?" "Should I be this way, or should I be that way?" It's a very clumsy and trying way to experience social interaction.

What continues to hinder me in the present is that I conceal how I feel. I don't often share my emotions with others. Similarly, I learned at an early age to hide the abuse; I learned how to appear as if everything was "normal," which was not being congruent with my feelings. While I continue to make an effort to prove how "normal" I am to the world, this is difficult — how do I know what "normal" is? Although I continue to present myself to the world this way, to feel safe, I'm also learning how to be congruent with others and have it feel okay.

I am just now experiencing developmental stage 4 and part of developmental stage 5. It is complex and perplexing to be learning now what I should have experienced as an adolescent. I feel so inadequate tackling my social skills this way, but I have nothing to fall back on, no education or experience in this area.

DORIS   The very opportunities that would have allowed Judy to develop normally at this age were denied her, not only by the restrictions placed upon her by her environment, but also by the development of her own inner family system of personalities. It was near or at this point that Judy lost her "self." What she has now are memories of events as experienced by "others," which is quite different from the actual "living out" of events as a singular person. Her ability to see herself as a competent person is affected by the losses of this very important developmental stage. Social skills can be copied, intellectual skills can be honed through education, but the solid inner knowledge of one's own self as a resource is missing.

Stage 5: Age 12 to 18 Years
(Adolescence)

DORIS   By the time Judy reached adolescence, she carried within her many personalities of varying ages, some dominant, some less dominant. The dominant personalities who were created to cope with the very chaotic and confusing stage of adolescence entered this stage unprepared for the demands of this period of development. These teenage personalities faced the same difficult tasks that all teenagers encounter: finding their own ego identity, interacting with their peers and "belonging" to a group, separating from family, and developing and exploring their own sexuality (see Table 4.5). Rather than develop as a "whole person," each dominant personality developed in a manner that was consistent with what each had learned to do to survive. For example, in order to keep the family secrets, there was a denial personality (Judith) who remained connected to the abusers to the very end of integration. A healthy separation from them was impossible. A social personality was created (Jane) to interact with peers, who used her abilities to observe and copy others as a means to access social skills. Although very intelligent, her ability to concentrate was fragmentary. She needed to remain vigilant at all times in order to do or say the "right thing." Even though she was a dominant personality, her time was not always her own, and she could not always control others who wanted to come out. This kind of chaos did not allow her to belong to a high-functioning group. Feelings of self-worth were affirmed neither by the abusers nor at school.

Development of one's own sexuality is another very important part of this stage of development. This only brought about more confusion. Negative, abusive sex had been Judy's constant companion since childhood. Sexuality and sex were one and the same. Sexual behavior at this stage of development conformed to that which had been learned. A sexual personality was created (Gerri) who acted out in negative and hurtful ways. Conflicts between personalities grew, amnestic barriers strengthened. The psychosocial tasks so important to healthy development could never be completed.

TABLE 4.5
Stage 5 (Age 12–18) of Normal Child Development and Development of MPD

Psychosocial Tasks	Healthy Parenting	Dysfunctional Parenting	Outcomes of Abuse for Child	MPD Development	Outcomes for MPD Adults
Ego identity Belonging to a group Separating from home Developing sexuality	Sets boundaries, but allows limits to extend as child's responsibleness increases Allows difference and disagreement *Messages* "We support you in your effort to discover yourself and be responsible for yourself." "We love you."	Constricting or nonexistent boundaries Symbiotic bond remains *Messages* "I don't care what you do." "I'll tell you what to do." "Get lost/go away." "Don't leave." "You'll never make it on your own." "You can't trust anyone but us."	Anxiety Lack of identity or several identities among various social groups Continued emotional enmeshment with abusers Extreme fluctuations in behavior and moods or compulsive conformity and overachievement Drug use Sexual problems Eating disorders	Dissociation and denial become necessary to cope with intense internal chaos and conflicts between personalities Amnestic barriers strengthen Dominant personalities develop autonomy Personality disorders may become encapsulated in personalities	"I don't know who I am, how I feel, or what I do." "I want to be whole, but I don't know how."

Columns 1–3 based on Erikson, 1950, and Clarke, 1978; columns 4–6 from Bryant et al., 1992, p. 47.

JUDY   I've barely entered into this developmental stage; I am just now finding out who I am. Belonging to a group, separating from the abusers, and exploring my own sexuality remain issues that I need to constantly address. Having lost earlier developmental stages complicates and makes completion of this stage more difficult.

The memories of experiences of integrated personalities were all I had in the beginning to identify who I was; it was the only history I had. Now I am finding out who *I* am, creating my own history, exploring and growing beyond my past, finding out there is more to me than just the memories of my integrated personalities. Now that I have a mind of my own, now that I don't dissociate and lose time, I am able to discover for myself what I can do and what I want for myself. Even though I am making progress, the loss of this developmental stage has created many difficulties for me in the present.

I feel inadequate with my own peers. I am extremely awkward, often sensing I don't belong. Emotionally, I perceive myself as much younger than my chronological age. This is when I experience the confusion between real and unreal. When what I see in the mirror doesn't correspond to the feelings I have about myself, I become confused. So when I am around my peer group I feel inadequate and vulnerable as though I have to pretend to be like them. My emotional age doesn't always correspond with my intellectual and chronological age. I become easily frustrated and embarrassed in situations where I am interacting with my peer group.

Separating from my abusers is another matter. Physical separation is no problem, but emotional separation is a continuing struggle. Emotional separation means I can no longer deny the abuse or the abusers' identities. Yet, I continue to wish for a resolution between myself and the abusers, which confuses me, for intellectually I know it is not possible.

Discovering my own sexuality is painful. I have so many memories of sexual abuse. I learned that my body was not lovely or beautiful, but an object to be abused. Claiming my femininity as positive is so difficult. To some degree I continue to disown my body. The disconnection makes the shame of sexual abuse less devastating.

Entering into this developmental stage at this time in my life is frustrating and sometimes a humiliating experience. And yet all I can do is continue to try to regain that which I have lost.

DORIS   The tumultuous world of the teenager is even more tumultuous when there has been little or no preparation for entry into that world. Physiological changes are occurring. Hormones are creating their own demands, even as teens are being asked to make responsible decisions about their future. Their desire to "belong" puts them under additional pressure from their peers as they search for their own ego identity.

Separating from home, experimenting with "new ways of being," and defining their sexuality while maintaining a healthy self-esteem requires the support of a stable and flexible family at home — one that has guided them through all the other developmental stages, laying a foundation for this very important stage. Even for adolescents who have that kind of background the psychosocial tasks demanded can seem overwhelming.

Judy herself did not live out this developmental stage; instead, she created a personality to carry out each separate task of this stage. To my knowledge, and to Judy's, none of these adolescent personalities were ever a part of earlier developmental stages. Integration, therefore, meant only the combining of different learnings and experiences, rather than developmental progression.

The focus of Judy's life during all developmental stages was learning how to survive within a restrictive, punishing, and closed environment. Activities outside this environment were limited and closely monitored, rules for behavior were strictly reinforced. Breaking any rule, particularly the rule about not revealing any family secrets, resulted in immediate and brutal punishment. While the ability to dissociate into many different personalities enabled her to cope with the abnormal life style she was forced to live, this same ability did not lend itself to development progression. A powerful determination to survive reinforced her ability to dissociate. The focus of her life was not personal growth, but personal survival. Given these circumstance normal developmental stages were either twisted and contaminated, or lost.

As Judy struggles to claim those developmental stages lost to her, she finds herself primarily alone. Even those closest to her have expectations of adult behavior and needs to be met. As a very responsible adult she does her best to meet those expectations and needs. At the same time, feelings of inadequacy and the need to hide those feelings behind a pretense of equanimity is a consistent drain of her energy.

Judy works on three levels at all times: (a) remembering, accepting, and coming to terms with the abuse and neglect in her past so that memories become history rather than an everyday presence; (b) acquainting herself with the losses of her childhood and the effect they now have in the present; and (c) cognitively working to replace those losses. In all these areas there is a factor of grief and anger. What comes easily to a child in those early years does not come easily to an adult. Judy cannot "start over." The road ahead promises to be a long and difficult one, but certainly one filled with numerous possibilities.

One of Judy's skills as a multiple was her ability to observe other people and their behaviors. She learned to use this skill in any manner of social situations as a means of hiding her own losses. This particular talent continues to be useful today for she has been able to use it in choosing role models for herself. In a sense, this has become the experiential part of life she missed because she has a chance to test her own experiences. Guidance comes through the feedback of her therapist and a few close friends. The safety of her home provides a retreat. The challenges are far from over, but Judy's own intelligence, courage, and determination to overcome all obstacles and to truly live will continue to be her greatest resources.

chapter 5

Ongoing Issues

The issues that had been addressed in therapy prior to integration continued to be addressed after integration. Before integration, each personality completed her own "individual" work and fused; as Judy moved closer to integration, each fusion meant she was now acquiring all the unfinished business each specific personality had carried. Once integration was accomplished, it became very clear that issues that had been problematic before integration would continue to be problematic after integration. Therefore, unlike her integrated personalities, Judy's work was far from finished. The path of post-integration was not to be an easy one for Judy, for although it was the result of remarkable personal achievement it was also one of personal sorrow.

The major issues involved those around acceptance of the abuse, including its extent as well as the identity of the abusers; continuing memories; and ongoing emotional, physical, and psychological pain, anger, and grief. The hope that the memories would fade quickly and the emotional and physical pain dissipate was not to be realized. Knowledge of her past, knowledge of those events that had contributed to the shattering of her personhood, and knowledge of the permanent damage she had suffered as a result of this past caused Judy to experience intense feelings of anger and grief. Denial no longer provided a safe haven—the memories were too clear; the depth of her anger was frighteningly intense, the subsequent depressions were depleting. Grief was a constant companion and it was within the context of grief work (Kübler-Ross, 1975) that Judy was able to express her feelings, acknowledge and accept her past. It was then that Judy was able to accept and mourn the tragedy of her own personal history. Acceptance, the last stage of grief, was the key that gave her the ability to see how her past encompassed every facet of her life, and it was acceptance that kept her out of denial and focused on the remaining work.

Acceptance of the Abuse

DORIS   One of Judy's major survival skills as a multiple was in her use of denial. Denial was exhibited in the form of personalities who were created to make things "okay," and/or to deny the abuse ever happened. In this way, she had some moments of comfort and could function in a world where it wasn't safe to talk about hearing voices or losing time.

Post-integration work meant accepting not only the fact that the abuse did occur but also the extent of the abuse. It meant memories of the abuse and the feelings about the abuse could no longer be dissociated. Feelings of rage, pain, depression, and deep sadness engulfed her. At times she felt overwhelmed by the tragedy of her own life. The fact that she had survived, that her struggle to integrate had been successful, was of little comfort to her during periods of intense grief. How could she accept the horror that had been her life? That kind of abuse was difficult for her to relate to in any way; it bore no semblance of reality to the way she lived her own life.

Confronting the truth, Judy had to look at her past—not as she wished it to be, but as it was. It took great courage to continue the confrontation, for as she began to accept the extent of her abuse she also had to accept that she could never have a normal relationship with those who abused her. At times, weary of the work confrontation entailed and seeking comfort, she would attempt to slip into her old survival habit of denial. These moments were short-lived as she found she was no longer able to deny the connection between her abusers and her past experiences.

JUDY   I was discouraged and disappointed to find I had so many issues still to deal with after integration, yet, at the same time, I was eager to have a more solid healing from the inside out as I encountered the continuing work.

My goal after integration was to become as healthy, functional, and empowered as was possible. This meant I had to confront the issues that remained, including acceptance of the abuse, continuation of memories, and looking at how I continued to use denial. Furthermore, I had to talk about my rage and anger, which was a part of my grief work. I had to grieve again for the losses I felt. In addition, I had to learn how to develop new patterns of coping with my continuing post-traumatic stress.

Consequently, one of the first issues I confronted was acceptance of the abuse; this was extremely difficult and has proven to be an ongoing struggle for me. Acceptance had to come on three different levels in order for the healing to take place: intellectually, emotionally, and physically.

Intellectually, I had accepted the extent to which I had been abused. Likewise, I had intellectually accepted that the abusers intentionally and maliciously abused me. As a result, I also had to acknowledge the identity of those who abused me. This was the most complex and heartrending aspect of the work. I just didn't want to believe who had abused me and yet it was necessary in order to free myself from the emotional bond with which I continued to struggle. I often asked, "How can I, on the one hand, intellectually accept the abuse, and yet, on the other hand, emotionally still be bonded to the abusers?" This was such a confusing and difficult problem to understand.

Consequently, the acceptance of my feelings of rage, shame, and humiliation helped loosen the emotional bond to the abusers. Once I allowed myself those feelings and I allowed myself to place the blame on the abusers, where it belonged, I was able to move forward. Every time I was able to accept the abuse, accept my own feelings, and not blame myself for the shame and humiliation I felt, I was less bound to those who had abused me. The struggle to believe and accept the truth was beginning to set me free.

In addition, I had to accept the reality of my ongoing health problems, the result of the extreme trauma that my body endured as a child; my body had been so terribly injured. It meant accepting that my future did not necessarily include good health. This was very hard. The truth is, I have had to learn how to make adjustments to living within the physical restrictions and limitations that remain a part of my life. In fact, my injuries, which include difficulty with asthma, back problems, and foot problems, remain constant reminders of the abuse.

Accepting the extent of the abuse I suffered has changed the way I will live the rest of my life. There is a freedom that comes with that acceptance; knowing why my body, emotions, and thoughts react in certain ways to particular situations. Acceptance has actually empowered me.

Accepting the abuse means living with the reality that there is nothing, *nothing*, in my personal world, in my personal relationships, in my whole life, that hasn't been touched by the abuse, whether it be a thought, a feeling, my actions, or reactions. Everything that I do has been touched by the abuse. When I accepted that, I was free to accept who I was.

DORIS   One of the more difficult results of integration for Judy is to have to continually confront the reality of the damage done by her abuse; emotionally, psychologically, and physically. Hopes that integration meant complete healing have been dashed. She now sees clearly how every area of her life has been affected.

Judy must monitor what she reads, what she watches on TV, and what movies she attends, for the triggers (see Chapter 7) still exist. The physical abuse she suffered as a child and young girl is beginning to take its toll. She is susceptible to many ills, and her energy resources are easily depleted. The nightmarish qualities of the first 18 years of her life continue to contaminate her sleeping and waking hours. Yet, the strength she has gathered from those parts of herself once separated and now fused is remarkable.

Just as she was determined to survive the abuse, she is as determined to make the most of every day of the life that is now her sole property: a life not shared with "others"; a life in which she now has choices; a life that is no longer one of utter chaos; a life in which she experiences a freedom she had never known. It is her acceptance of the experiences of her lifetime that has given her this freedom, for she no longer blames herself for all the broken pieces of her life. She is now able to know and to understand how destructive abuse can be to the human psyche, and yet, she is not destroyed. This knowledge has empowered and released her from the self-destructive beliefs that held her captive for so many years.

Continuation of Memories

JUDY   Memories continued to emerge after integration, but the rate and intensity of the memories changed, as did the way in which I dealt with the feelings and information from them.

In retrospect, I now believe that remembering my past was the single most important element in reaching total integration. It allowed me to enter the world I had dissociated from and bring it to my conscious awareness. Indeed, it enabled me to relive those memories and observe moments from my past and utilize them as important therapeutic tools.

Since integration, I've gained a new perspective while working on memories. I no longer experience or relive the memories as a frightened child; instead, I experience them as an adult. This new perspective helped me remove the negative beliefs I once owned — that I was responsible for the abuse or somehow deserved the abuse. Through my adult eyes I was able to perceive clearly how the abusers used and punished the helpless child I once was. And with this new adult perspective, the self-blame turned into understanding.

Memories released to me by my integrated personalities stimulated the recall of other memories and I experienced them with all the feelings I had gained through integration. In the first stage of post-integration, this was very difficult and frightening, since I had never felt that type of intensity of feelings before. Yet, there was a turning point for me when I knew, truly knew and believed, that I could feel those feelings without the fear of death. In other words, I had already stared death in the face as a child and survived, and knowing I survived that amount of pain gave me the courage I needed to continue. And although the feelings were intense, they were not like the actual events I experienced as a child because now I had supportive people in my life and therapists who could help me work through these issues. As a result, I was now, more than ever, ready and able to deal with the continuing memories.

DORIS   Of major importance for Judy at this time in her life was the fact she had the security of knowing that her immediate family and close friends would be there to provide her with a solid and committed support system—a support system she was surely going to need during the rocky times that lay ahead, for Judy's reentry into the world as her "self" meant owning all the memories and feelings long carried by her other personalities. The memories brought with them feelings that were particularly intense. As she had no other prior experience as her self to measure these feelings against, it was as if she was meeting them head-on for the first time. As a child and young girl, these feelings had been connected with torture and fear of death—fears so intense they led to immobilization and dissociation. When these memories and feelings emerged, she was able to acknowledge intellectually that the memories belonged to the past, although she was still unable to control the feelings attached to the memories. The feelings continued to plague her, taking on the form of immobilizing anxiety attacks and nightmares. Even so there was a difference, for now she was able to make a connection between the two. She now knew where those feelings came from, and she could understand why they were so intense. This information did not decrease the intensity of the feelings but it did give Judy a point of reference; she knew she had possessed the strength she needed to survive her torturous past experiences, and it was a strength she could still draw from to survive the memories of the past.

JUDY   In stage 2 of post-integration, memories continued to surface. They were like bits and pieces of dissociated information. Not major pieces, but ones I needed to remember to fill out the memories I'd already recovered, to give them more detail. And yet, I still found it difficult to totally own them as mine. I would project the memories of my past onto one of the integrated personalities, often saying, "I remember that memory but it was Judith who lived through that." In that way I was still able to distance myself from the newly acquired information I had gained through integration; I was able to feel safe and protect myself from having an intense experience that I was not able to cope with at that point in time.

I used dissociation in therapy to recall the memories yet to be reclaimed. I did this myself, feeling very much in charge of my own work. I would put myself into a trance-state like the trance-state I was originally in when I experienced the abuse as a child. I had not yet learned any other way to bring up and discuss the remaining material.

DORIS   Judy's ability to use a trance-state to complete her memory work was invaluable. This ability allowed her to have control over her own discoveries, to retrieve only what she was able to accept at that particular moment in time, and to begin to put the pieces of the puzzle of her many memories together. It was heartbreaking and exhausting work, for there were many, many pieces and the pictures that emerged were ugly. Real progress was made when she stopped projecting past experiences on her former personalities and claimed them as her own. The fear that the use of trance would negate her integration was gone.

JUDY   The memories changed in the latter part of stage 3 of post-integration therapy. It was no longer like a flashback of traumatic events that I relived and abreacted, but a remembering. I now remembered memories while I remained in the present and the memories remained as something of my past. It's like acknowledging the past without having to live through it again.

In fact, not all the information that was surfacing was negative. What I was remembering were small bits of information — not unlike other people who have triggers that cause them to remember something from their childhood — a sight, a smell, or a sound. For example, I would recall the color of the chair in my room as a child or the color of a blanket that was on my bed. Besides the memories released to me by each personality as they integrated and the memories I continued to recall on my own, I was now remembering specific events in therapy; events that had occurred during the time I was a multiple and still in a dissociative state. Again these were positive experiences, for example, having a picnic or experiencing the beach for the first time, as a child would. Having conversations with my therapists on philosophical issues, as a young adult would.

These continuing memories of experiences with my therapists — their kind words, their reassurance, their gentle ways — were also becoming a part of "my" life experience. The consistent, secure, and accepting environment in therapy I experienced as a multiple allowed me now, as integrated, to believe for myself that I could trust in others outside of myself, that there was goodness in the world to be found and experienced. As I continued to remember the contact my personalities had with my therapists during therapy, I realized how much I had gained from those experiences.

Even more important was how I began to accept the memories and conceptualize the information as belonging to me. It was a major change as I shifted into actually seeing the memories as mine — not as experiences of the integrated personalities. As a result of this change, I continued to be affected by post-traumatic stress. Since I was no longer isolating the feelings or dissociating from them, and I was now dealing with everything (the memories, the history, the grief, and my body), my body reacted. My whole body felt the pain of remembering. I became sorely aware of how much abuse my body had taken by the amount of pain I carried with those memories. This was a major turning point in how I experienced the remaining information that would surface during the latter part of my post-integration therapy.

DORIS   Retrieval of memories brought with it not only emotional and psychological pain, but physical pain as well. In order to survive the abuse Judy encountered as a child and young girl, she learned to dissociate from pain, to create parts of herself to hold pain for her, and in so doing separated the pain from the memory. She had always connected the aches, the pains, and the asthma she suffered in her adult life with everyday events, such as strained muscles from yard work or "female problems" or allergies, although at times the pain could be intense and unexplainable. With the retrieval of memories, the memories and pain were once more connected. The pain of remembering now included her whole being. Post-traumatic stress took the place of dissociation.

As each memory was complete, when all the pieces were in place,

Judy no longer experienced them in such a traumatic fashion. She could acknowledge them as memories, something *remembered*, something from her past, not something that was likely to spring up unexpectedly to haunt her in the present with flashbacks, night terrors, and inexplicable physical pain. Disturbing though these memories might be, they were her history and she now had a clear picture of who she was and how she came to be. When she was able to claim her history she was able to reclaim her life.

Ongoing Grief

JUDY   When I was young, I could not safely express any feelings; not anger at the atrocities, not pain for the physical hurt, not depression or sadness for the things I longed for. There was no one in my life to help support the expression of those feelings I had as a child, no one. As a child, I believed that if I broke down and felt these feelings, I would become weak, unable to survive what I must. Denying my feelings was the only way to be strong; to survive the unsurvivable.

As an adult multiple, I learned that I could continue to dissociate the feelings. After integration, when I gained my feelings back I felt overwhelmed by them. The grief particularly was agony for me. To simply feel any of my feelings was like a trigger. But when the feelings of sadness and anger were so great they seemed to consume me, I would actually think I was going to die. As a result, even after integration, I would find a way to deny these feelings until they built up inside like a bomb ready to explode.

I would distract myself by staying busy to the point of exhaustion. This was an excellent way, I thought, to cover up the feelings, which were just sitting below the surface. I held these feelings so deep inside for so many years that I found they were always waiting close by, waiting to be expressed. I hadn't realized how much I needed to honor the feelings I kept buried and hidden from myself until they did explode in such force that I became blinded by the fury of my anger or so depressed by the deep sadness. I was then forced to acknowledge them.

Just as difficult was being able to share feelings of great sadness or anger with my family and friends. It was as if I needed to protect them from my pain. Denial of my grief kept me from telling them the truth of how much pain I was experiencing. It kept me from telling them the truth of how badly I was abused as a child, and how badly my feelings of rage and sadness sat inside, festering like an open wound. How could I fulfill the roles of wife, mother, and friend, that I believed were expected of me, when I had all these feelings that I had to deal with? I didn't know how to achieve a balance between family and feelings. And I worried and questioned, "If I express my feelings will my family and friends still be supportive of me?" "Will they understand?" I was too afraid to share with them—afraid at this point they might abandon me. It was a great risk to express my pain to them.

As I worked at releasing my sadness and feelings of hurt, it was like I had a valve that I could turn off and on. I would let it out a little at a time, crying for only a small time, then go back to feeling numb again. I would shift back into feeling safe not expressing the grief. Day by day as I opened the valve a little more and released my feelings, I began to cry more each day until I was crying all the time; at home, in therapy, with my family, by myself, over breakfast, at the grocery store, at night. It just didn't matter where I was; the tears began to flow so heavily I just couldn't turn off the valve. I cried until my eyes were so swollen they hurt and stung as the tears streamed down my face. I cried until I was exhausted.

Once I allowed these feelings to be expressed, I realized they weren't as dangerous as I once believed. I wasn't afraid any longer to allow them to be a part of who I was. The more I allowed my sadness to be expressed, the easier it got. I was less afraid of expressing grief. And even though I was in a lot of pain, there was also a feeling of relief.

DORIS   Judy's ability to dissociate from her feelings was no longer an option. The memories she had put together piece by piece helped her to make sense of her life but they did nothing to assuage her grief. The memories themselves were a causality. At this time Judy particularly needed the support and understanding of her family and friends. Since she rarely allowed herself to express feelings of sorrow, rage, and despair outside the therapeutic setting, she was uncertain as to how such feelings would be received; she was also fearful that the intensity would be misunderstood, that she would lose control, and that she would be consumed by feelings. It was difficult for her to believe that the expression of these feelings was not only acceptable but also essential—even now she struggled with old learnings from her childhood: Never show feelings of anger, fear, pain, or sadness, or punishment will surely follow. Punishment now would mean loss of family and friends. Learning that she was following the normal pattern of grief, that there were different stages she would encounter, and that experiencing and expressing feelings was an important part of healing helped her to release emotions that had been pent up for so long. The tears she had never shed, tears that expressed the sorrow of her many losses, tears that offered release from years of unexpressed grief, seemed endless. She found that the support she needed from family and friends was available; she no longer needed to fear punishment or loss for experiencing and expressing her deepest emotions.

JUDY   As my grief continued, the tears turned into a rage so overwhelming that I became confused with feelings of guilt and fear. I felt angry at myself, at my friends, at my therapists, at anyone who was in my life, at any situation I was a part of. I felt guilt for feeling such anger. I was confused about what anger was. I was afraid of my anger because I thought it meant I was a violent person. What I wasn't doing was focusing the anger around my many losses, and at the abusers, by whom I felt so betrayed. Rather than directing my anger where it belonged, I was lashing out at everybody and everything.

It was a struggle to express my anger, but once I did I was raging mad at all my losses: all the time I lived as a multiple trying to cope with the abuse, for the time it was taking even after integration to deal with the damage done, for all the years I'd lost and had to work to regain, for my loss of innocence, for all the moments of pleasure I missed experiencing. I was angry for not being protected, not having a family, not being held or nurtured. I was so angry about what I could have been if given the opportunities to grow as a normal child. There seemed to be no end to the losses I felt and at the anger that needed to be expressed. It felt like a huge steel ball rolling around inside my stomach, crushing me as I tried to breathe; it weighed so heavy on my heart that I thought it would break and I would surely die.

I continued to work on understanding my anger and accepting

that anger could be an ordinary part of my life—expressing it, not penning it up, letting it be part of my many feelings, and using it as a tool for action. While working at this stage of my grief I began to experience anger as a valuable gift. I was learning to use it to see the truth of the abuse, to understand the reality I must live, and to experience the truth of my real feelings. Anger refused to let me stay in denial. Anger was clearing the way for self-acceptance, allowing me to nurture my pain, and giving me strength for action against the injustices I had experienced. This information has proved to be invaluable to me, for what I learned at this stage was that anger is not the monster I once believed it to be; rather, it is a positive expression of the pain I needed to express.

DORIS   This stage of Judy's grief work was the most difficult for her. She did not see anger as useful and healthy. She had learned at a very early age never to express an emotion that was not acceptable to her abusers, for that would bring immediate punishment. The anger over her abuse and those who had abused her had been split off to be carried by other personalities. Once she was integrated, she began the process of claiming that anger as her own, and the intensity of that anger frightened her. Her experience with the anger of others in her early years had taught her that the primary expression of anger was violence and loss of control, the consequences of which, for her, were abuse, pain, and violation. Once she got in touch with the depth of her anger, she struggled to find a way to express it in a way that was acceptable to her, a way that would not mirror the behavior of her abusers.

At first, it was difficult for her to keep her anger focused since she wasn't ready to place the anger where it belonged—on the abusers. That was still too frightening; she was only beginning to believe she had the "right" to be angry, let alone be angry at those who taught her she was never, at any time, to show anger, let alone express it. So what Judy did at this point was a normal response to angry feelings when combined with feelings of powerlessness—she displaced it.

The recipients of her anger became those she felt safest with: her therapists, family, and friends. It was a difficult yet productive time, for these encounters enabled her to "practice" communicating anger in nondestructive ways and affirmed her "right" to feel anger. Judy found out what she needed to know: She did not "go out of control," she was not a violent person, and she had control of her behavior even in anger. She could now focus her anger where it belonged: on those who were responsible for her many losses. Anger was an emotion she no longer feared.

JUDY   As I expressed the pain, the sadness, and rage, I also continued to wish for those things I knew I could never change. I longed for the apologies I would never hear. I tried to make sense out of my life, and I still continued to ask, "Why did this happen to me?"

It always came back to acceptance, to see the truth for what it was. I had to let go of the wishing to stay on task with living. I had to finally let go of my fantasy of dreams that would never become true. I could not change what was, nor could I wish it into existence. I learned that the more I focused on what I wished I had had, the more depressed I became and the less I was able to express my anger and pain. I would then slip back into holding those wishes inside as if I could somehow make them true.

Grief is an ongoing feeling for me. It is rather like an ache that is always there. Sometimes I am able to put it away, sometimes not. It seems to cycle around from acceptance to sadness to anger to depression, and sometimes even to denial. But no matter what stage of grief I am in, there is always an underlying feeling of sadness that sits inside, that remains a part of who I am. I don't always express it any more, but I know that it is there, and I am always aware of it.

DORIS   Judy continued to swing between denial and acceptance. She neither denied that the abuse occurred nor absolved the abusers; instead, she managed to push feelings away, wanting to spend her days concentrating on creating a future rather than being constantly reminded of the past. Rage was never far from the surface. She was tired of therapy, she was tired of hurting, she was tired of remembering. She longed for that which she could not have: changes in those who had so cruelly abused her, acknowledgement by them of that cruelty. Yet, no matter how she viewed her situation, no matter what attempts she made to see those cruel ones in a different context or interact with them differently, their behaviors did not change. Their personalities did not change. The knowledge that there was no hope for any kind of relationship, that her losses were permanent, brought with it depression and a deep sense of sadness. There was no way to erase the memories, no way to change the past. It was a time for mourning, a time to let go, and finally, a time to accept that her history would continue to impact the rest of her life and that she would never be totally free of the grieving.

Reconnecting with the Body

JUDY   Integration brought physical sensations I had not experienced before. Physical feelings were not something that I chose to experience, but were a natural process that came as I integrated each personality. As sensations returned to my body, I began to feel my arms, my legs, my back; all of me. I was now connected with the body that I had dissociated from and disowned for over 38 years— *my body*. As a result, during post-integration I was left with the challenge of dealing with the many issues that came up around having reconnected with my body: accepting my body, feeling visible, being female, and taking care of my body.

I began slowly to allow myself to experience the feelings within my body by paying more attention to the physical sensations I had while doing ordinary daily activities like brushing my teeth, washing my face, bathing, or even breathing. I no longer numbed out the physical sensations I had avoided for years. This was a nonthreatening way to begin to accept my body the way it was.

Initially it was even difficult to look at my body. It was like looking at the body of a stranger. I needed to acquaint myself with my own body, the body I had lost years ago. It was no longer the body of the child I remembered; it was the body of a woman. As I explored my body, looking at it in the mirror, I began to understand how the abuse had caused permanent injuries. And, as I touched my body, I was reminded of the pain I felt; the pain my body had sustained for so many years, the pain I was beginning to feel. I thought, "My God, my body has felt this pain for all these years." To realize that I had never felt or comforted the pain was a shocking realization.

The most difficult issue I had to accept was that I would never have the opportunity to be young or to have the body of a young person. This was extremely painful as I again longed for what I could never have. Wanting to experience being youthful, yet knowing I was connected to a body of a woman, to a body that had been damaged and injured, to a body that seemed old and in pain, I was again faced with mourning a loss, one that I would never regain.

Learning to accept my body was indeed difficult, but it was even more difficult to like my body, to not hate it any longer. I had felt betrayed by my body and I had despised it, blaming my body for responding to sexual stimulation, for being a female body, for being so vulnerable, for just *being*. Changing that pattern of thinking was a major turning point. I did this by acknowledging and affirming the strength of my body and its ability to get through the horrendous abuse put upon it. I began by saying, "Wasn't it good that my body was able to survive the abuse, that it was strong enough to allow me to live?" By affirming this one thing, I began to realize my body had been an ally, a friend who had been the container of the pain I never allowed myself to feel or experience as a child. Consequently, I could no longer ignore the fact that my body needed to be nurtured and to be seen as something worth taking care of, that *I* was worth taking care of.

Even more important was learning how to treat my body with care and consideration. This was a new experience for me. It meant I would have to begin to listen to my body and not ignore it. Previously, when I was cold, I would ignore the feeling, thinking it was not worth the effort to put on warm clothing. When I was sick, I ignored resting and caring for myself. When my back ached with pain, I never took the time to ease the pain or to comfort the feeling. In fact, since I never thought of my body as a part of me, I never thought of my body as important.

I now listen and respond to the needs of my body. I have given my body respect and I now know that my body is important. I now see my body as much a part of who I am as my feelings, emotions, and intellect. I've also learned that my body is a great source of knowledge and information and listening to my body's messages has allowed me to maintain better physical health. It has allowed me to experience life again. And although this means feeling pain sometimes, I realize this is a vital connection to living.

DORIS   As integration progressed and physical feelings began to return to Judy's body, she could no longer deny its existence.

As her mind released memories, her body also released memories: memories of the abuse her body had suffered. Memories she had been able to dissociate for many years began to return. The return was painful because the parts of her body that had been so terribly wounded now cried out to be recognized. Mind and body now worked together to eliminate any residual denial of that abuse, which was an important factor for the wholeness Judy desired. Reframing the purpose of pain was an essential but difficult part of therapy.

To experience her body as a living, breathing organism that was sensitive to touch and responsive to environmental changes and to many other sensations was to become a newly accepted part of Judy's post-integration work. After avoiding her body for years through dissociation, seeing it as a betrayer of her "self," she now began to look at it with new eyes. She began to see that her body had sustained her through many horrifying ordeals; its strength enabled her to survive.

Now, even as it reminded her of its wounding, it also asked to be nurtured. No longer separated from her physical self, Judy found that in responding to the needs of her body she was also responding to her own need for nurturance. This knowledge continued to strengthen the connection, enabling her to accept her body as an integral part of her "self."

With this acceptance also came the need to accept herself as female and as a woman. To learn that being female was not ugly and shameful, but rather a vital and powerful part of who she was, became an important aspect of Judy's post-integration therapy. Mourning the loss of never having been able to enjoy and experience a healthy, youthful body was a part of this work. For Judy, being a woman now means to accept and respect the woman she is in the present without ever having made the journey from childhood to womanhood herself. Acceptance, is an ongoing part of Judy's post-integration work.

JUDY   Feelings of extreme visibility came as I connected with my body. I was really "out there," I thought. And, being seen, I felt so vulnerable — not that I was being viewed by other people, but that I was being seen as a female, and female meant sexual. I panicked. I didn't want people to see me as sexual. I had learned from my childhood that being female meant I could be used sexually; I could be abused in a sexual way. Consequently, I was very fearful about being seen as female. I had many angry feelings about being a female, about being abused because I was a female. I've had to accept being female as something I can't change. Being female is something I want to learn to enjoy. I'm still working on this.

Slowly I've allowed myself to explore and discover my femininity. I began by wearing clothes that made me more attractive, wearing make-up, and wearing my hair in a more stylish way. Taking the risk of expressing my femininity made me feel vulnerable; it was frightening at first. Slowly I allowed myself to further express my femininity with those I trusted the most and in social situations in which I felt safe. I couldn't risk doing this in public unless I had those around me for support; it was a long time before I could do this on my own.

Getting in touch with my feminine side also gave me a different point of view about my sexuality as a woman. I'm beginning to learn to appreciate my sexuality and sex is now something I can experience in a different way. I can now experience sex with someone I love and who loves me; I now know it is an expression of my husband's caring that I experience.

DORIS   Once Judy was integrated she could no longer hide "inside." Being visible was a new experience for her as well as a painful one. In the past, being seen had meant objectification and abuse, being humiliated and shamed. With no place to hide any longer, she had to learn new ways to shelter herself. One of these ways was to allow her angry feelings to surface; the depth of her anger brought with it a sense of power, which strengthened her ability to build personal boundaries.

She learned she had to create a whole new picture of herself for herself, unlearning what she had learned about that "self" in the past and find, in the present, the meaning of her own femininity. At all times in this process she battled her fears of visibility. In the first phase of post-integration, even the simple act of curling her hair was frightening for she thought curly hair would make her more visible.

Learning to appreciate herself as a female and as feminine is an ongoing process for Judy. By setting her own pace and carefully choosing what risks she's willing to take, she is able to create some safety for herself. Her own successes and the impact of positive women role models in her life continue to affirm her as a woman and encourage her in this undertaking.

JUDY   In brief, acceptance of my body has meant that I accept my body the way it is, and affirm the fact that my body was initially very strong and that is why I survived. I must also accept that it has been injured permanently and that it will never completely heal. Once I accepted these facts, I began to look at what I could change and learn to accept what I couldn't. The difference now is that I can choose what I want to do with my body, how I want to move my body, use my body, and care for my body.

I now have the opportunity to decide whether I want to do anything with my body image — my appearance. Do I choose to lose weight? Do I find my appearance to be acceptable or unacceptable? I now have the opportunity to decide whether I want to do anything about my health. Do I want to quit smoking? I am in total control of my body now. And no matter what I've decided to do around any of these issues, I've accepted my decisions as okay. And there is no guilt that I lay on myself for those decisions.

One of the hardest things I have done in post-integration was to bring this last part of myself *into* myself, that is, reconnect with my body and see it as part of the whole, that I am now truly a whole person, that there is no longer a separation, and that I can have a loving relationship with my entire self. As a result, I now feel a sense of self-esteem. I'm learning to see the good things about my body. I'm learning to have a more gentle and loving relationship with myself, all of me, completely. It means the whole of me: my body, mind, and spirit.

DORIS   The circle can be used as a symbol of wholeness, of completeness. If a circle were used to symbolize Judy's life prior to integration, the picture would be a circle broken into many pieces. When Judy entered therapy, she began the painstaking and painful work of putting those many broken pieces back together. Reconnecting with the body was the last piece of the circle to be put in place. The circle is now complete. Judy is whole.

However, the acceptance of this last piece was not easy, for it meant Judy must acknowledge the permanent damage that had been done to her body. Damage in other aspects of her life was difficult enough to accept, but her body continues to be a constant reminder of the abuse, whether it is the pain she still suffers daily in many parts of her body or the body image that somehow seems incongruent with the period of time she has been in the world. She has chosen to accept this as a part of her life and use it as her own bill of rights, rights never before available to her: the right to care for her body, the right to appreciate her body, and the right to create and maintain personal space as it fits for her.

chapter 6

Developing New
Patterns of Coping

The coming together of all of Judy's many disowned personalities brought the work that lay ahead for her even more sharply into focus. Now that she was living in the world "on her own" she needed to continue to develop resources that enlarged her view of the world and her place in it. This meant continuing to work not only on those areas connected with lost developmental stages, but also on present-day issues. It was her awareness of how the past continued to contaminate the present that helped her work through this tangled web. The knowledge that there had been nothing in her past that had prepared her for living in the world as she now knew it helped her come to terms with all the difficulties she was experiencing in the present. She was now able to accept what she had found so difficult to accept; that in many ways, even though she was now an adult, her learnings would be those that she should have had the opportunities to explore in her childhood years.

92

Learning to Trust

DORIS   Prior to integration, even as we dealt with the many difficult issues that multiple personality disorder presents, I kept a continuous focus on building trust. Trust became the "connector" between all her separated parts; trust was the connector between those parts and the therapists; and trust, after integration, proved to have been the foundation upon which integration had been built.

Trust in her therapists created the safe environment Judy needed to examine her own perceptions of past and present experiences. She began to feel safe enough to explore her own boundaries and feelings, and to express her needs. She now used her time in therapy for the kind of feedback that validated the authenticity of her present-day experiences as well as her memories of the past.

The work she had done in therapy to develop her own inner resources was proving to be solid. Her therapists remained her primary outside resource for guidance and support and yet she was beginning to rely more and more on her own judgment. The element of trust, which played such a powerful role in the process of integration, now revealed itself in a new and even more powerful capacity. Judy was beginning to trust herself. It was during stage 3 of her post-integration work that she began to focus on and develop new and more efficacious coping patterns, patterns that fit with her own personal growth and present way of life.

JUDY   Trust was the foundation on which I built everything. I had built a solid foundation of trust in therapy and I learned to trust not only in myself, but also in others. In fact, this basic sense of safety was the necessary component needed to reach beyond my old ways of coping and discover and use new ways to deal with my life as an integrated person.

Learning to trust myself was most important; trusting what I saw, what I heard, and what I felt as real and true was extremely hard and demanding work, as it went against all the old messages not to trust anything at all. With continuous feedback, validation, and support from my therapists I was able to trust in my own perceptions and experiences.

In addition, as my trust level grew in therapy I was more able to trust in others and in my environment. In fact, the trust I had built was the basis for taking new risks in the world. I felt safe taking what I learned in therapy to the world outside. I was reaching beyond the trust I had built between my therapists and myself to others outside, including my family, my friends, and others in my environment.

I found that trust was a skill I could learn and use. In fact, it opened up a passageway to accessing and learning new coping skills. Trust allowed me to gain more control over my life. In addition, it taught me that I could take more responsibility for myself. Trust gave me the ability to make choices and sound decisions. Finally, trust gave me the confidence that I needed to express my feelings and needs, to move beyond the walls of isolation and silence I had built around myself as a multiple. Trust gave me the freedom to grow.

DORIS   Judy's life experiences had not taught her to trust either herself or others. Her early years were involved with people who deliberately sought to confuse her; they confused her to the degree that she could never be sure that what she saw, heard, or felt was a reality. It was only within the safety of the therapeutic setting, beginning with the pre-integration period, that she learned the meaning of trust.

Judy had to trust her therapists before she could trust her feedback, which confirmed the truth of what she was seeing, hearing, and feeling. It was this feedback, proof that her therapists believed and trusted her, that helped her to begin to trust herself. She began to believe the truths her therapists reflected back to her, that she had within herself the strength, the wisdom, and the ability to change her world.

Setting Boundaries

DORIS   As Judy's trust in her own abilities to cope with internal and external factors grew so did her desire to expand her world. She had established a place of safety within her home, with her family, and with her friends. She was now ready to explore the world and her place in it within a context never before available to her; a world where she set the boundaries for her own involvement; a world filled with new possibilities. Her newly established sense of safety gave her the security she needed to take risks, to explore new options, and to continue to refine or redesign the coping skills she found most useful.

Her ability to define her own boundaries was a major importance in the area of coping. She was raised within a system that had allowed her no boundaries and no personal space. The only boundaries she knew were the rock-solid walls her abusers erected whenever she had a need for comfort or an escape from pain. Otherwise, boundaries were whatever might be dictated in the moment or for a particular event. There was no consistency. Because of these early experiences, boundaries in the realm of interpersonal relationships proved to be an area that required new learnings on Judy's part: first, that she had a right to personal space; second, that other people's personal space wasn't a brick wall even though it might feel that way; and third, that she had a right to set boundaries for herself in ways that met her needs and brought her security.

At first Judy felt very uncomfortable setting boundaries. Her experimentation in this area sometimes left her feeling confused and isolated. She had to learn the difference between healthy contact and intrusiveness, which was very difficult to learn because there was so much to unlearn. Once she learned, however, once she found there was security and strength in claiming her own personal space, she was able to see the importance of that need in others. This new knowledge made it possible for her to contact others in a new way and continues to enrich her interpersonal relationships. She thus added a new measure of protection for herself and a new measure of awareness, which added to her ability to explore many more options for her life.

JUDY   I never felt comfortable saying, "No." All I knew was that if someone wanted something, anything from me, they could take it. In addition, I never interpreted my time as my own or ever considered putting myself first. Yet, as I learned to trust and listen to myself, including my ideas and my decisions, I began to see I could set my own limits and boundaries.

It was also necessary to learn about my personal body space in order to feel secure and safe, yet I had no idea where to begin. I started by making a mental list of what I wanted for myself and my body; what was most comfortable and what was off limits to others. What was most difficult was asserting those rights and limits; it felt awkward since I had never voiced such clear boundaries before, but with each new attempt I felt both a new sense of protection as well as a growing belief in my right to have boundaries.

Next, I learned how to set boundaries in relationships. I learned I didn't have to do all the giving or all the receiving; there had to be a balance between the two. I learned I could say no to my friends and have them say no to me and not feel guilty, rejected, or rejecting in either situation. In fact, I learned that it took both people in the relationship to make it work—not just me.

Since I hadn't had much practice setting limits and boundaries it took a lot of practice. Just as important, I had to learn to be flexible; I had to learn to negotiate and compromise, to meet other people half way.

Although setting boundaries was difficult at first, I found it had its rewards. I felt safer because I could protect myself from situations I did not want to be in. I could get more of my needs met and I could meet other people's needs without going beyond my limits. As a result, I felt more respect for myself and experienced more respect from other people. And any time I felt selfish sticking to my boundaries, I reminded myself, "Judy, you are *not* selfish, you are taking care of yourself and your needs."

Expressing Feelings and Needs

DORIS   The challenges that post-integration brought for Judy were not easily addressed. There were so many feelings; feelings that seemed to tumble over one another giving little time to sort them out and no advance notice as to what would be coming up next. The work done in therapy prior to integration did not automatically lend itself to these new challenges.

Judy believed that all the work she had done in the past would have equipped her to take control, to be "in charge" of her feelings. She hadn't counted on the chaos she was to experience when she became "sole owner" of those feelings, and fell back into old patterns of blaming herself and feeling bad for not being able to express her feelings "appropriately." Her self-esteem tumbled.

During these difficult times Judy learned that these feelings were not only connected to past memories, but were also indicators of the many new experiences she was encountering in the present. The chaos became much more understandable. As she began to accept the fact that chaos was a "normal" reaction to the flood of feelings and memories that came her way and an important part of post-integration, she stopped blaming herself.

Sorting out which feelings were connected to the past, which were connected to the present, and understanding how the past continued to contaminate the present became an important part of therapy. Each connection strengthened Judy's confidence in her ability to make further connections. In this way, step by step, she was able to more clearly place her feelings within their proper context and with each placement she gained new understanding and control.

Judy also learned how closely her feelings and needs are connected. Feelings arose out of needs and needs arose out of feelings. The loss of so many early developmental stages had left her ill-prepared to express either and so it was a matter of learning within the safety of the therapeutic setting the basics of expressing both. Her increased ability to be in control of her feelings provided the balance needed for expression of both. Her range of choices increased and she became aware of new possibilities. For instance, in the past, anger was a "bad" feeling to be stuffed down and ignored; now she could choose whether to express her anger. She could be as creative as she wished in her expression of it. She found she no longer thought of her anger as "bad," to be feared because it might go out of control, nor did she label herself as a "bad person" for having angry feelings. Anger had become an important source of healthy energy.

Expressing her needs proved to be more difficult. As a child she had learned that only the needs of others were important, and any expression of her needs would mean quick and severe punishment and rejection. Over the years of continuing abuse, denial of her own needs became a part of her defense. The power of this kind of negative reinforcement proved to be a real stumbling block in the first phases of post-integration. It was difficult for her to separate past from present; to accept she had needs, let alone ask that they be met. Cognitively she could accept that having needs was a part of the human experience, but fears of punishment and rejection deeply embedded from her past would not let her claim those needs for herself. It was within the safety of the therapeutic setting, with therapists* she could trust, that she continued the hard work of separating past experiences from present realities. She learned to look at each need and accept that each need was rooted in a child-hood loss. She understood how the contamination of past feelings served to intensify present feelings and invalidate her experiences of present-day situations. She allowed herself to grieve her many losses and to accept the validity of her needs. Once she had ac-cepted their validity she was able to begin the difficult task of learn-ing how to meet those needs in spite of her fears.

JUDY   Integration brought an onslaught of feelings; feelings I had never allowed myself to experience before. At first, I was in total chaos, feeling overwhelmed by the flooding of enormous emotions. However, I was working hard in post-integration therapy to learn how to feel those feelings as well as to separate them from past and present experiences.

In an effort to see how old feelings still contaminated present-day feelings, I began to pay more attention to the reasons I was having the feelings in the first place. For example, when I experienced strong feelings I would ask myself, "Why am I having this feeling? Does it fit this situation?" It was like having a reality checklist. If the feeling fit, I felt almost relieved and more comfortable. But if the feeling and the situation did not match, I felt confused; I would then have to look for connections between them.

There were always answers to why I was experiencing those feel-ings. Usually I found that the connection was a trigger; something in the present that reminded me of a past experience and would thus cause old feelings to surface. It was always reassuring to under-stand why I felt a certain way and to understand where the feelings

---

*Lynda Shirar was cotherapist at this time.

originated from. But this wasn't always possible, and I couldn't always figure them out. It was at this point that it became necessary to talk about those feelings in therapy; it was just as important to express the confusion I had about those feelings and still get the permission I needed to be able to feel.

The safety and trust I built in therapy allowed me to express my feelings, and the constant validation reassured me that there were no good or bad feelings, but that feelings were just that: feelings. Through example and feedback I learned that it was not only okay to talk about feelings, but that it was also important for me to do that. At the same time, this was a major struggle for me as I would vacillate between feeling as if I could express them safely and not believing it was safe to do so.

Accordingly, I would often fall into my old pattern of pretending everything was fine while feeling totally overwhelmed with depression, anger, or sadness. I had learned so well how not to express what I felt that it took practice and more practice to be congruent. In addition, I learned there was no single way to show emotions or talk about them; I had to learn how to communicate them in a way that could be heard and understood. As a result, I began to see how certain ways of communicating my feelings increased the likelihood that I could have my needs met.

Furthermore, as I learned to express my needs I felt vulnerable to old feelings of shame and guilt. "Was I worthy of having my needs met?" "Was it my fault if they weren't?" These were questions I constantly struggled with and which were often accompanied by negative self-talk and blaming. To overcome these feelings and thoughts, I would state out loud over and over to myself that I was allowed to have needs. For example, I would say, "Judy you *do* feel bad and you deserve to be heard." I had to make the effort to bring it from inside of myself to the outside and look at it in a way that could be validated. I also had to learn to hear others when they were validating or supporting my feelings. Consequently, it was like opening up my ears and hearing for the first time that I was justified in having the needs and the feelings I was experiencing. As a result, I now had the impetus I needed to continue sharing my needs without guilt, shame, or the fear of rejection.

I slowly gained the ability to express my needs and to experiment asking for support during hard or frightening times. For example, I would say, "This is how I feel, this is what is happening inside of me, this is what my experience is, and this is what I need." In this way, I learned to share feelings and talk about them in a way that enriched not only myself but my friendships as well. And although I felt shaky at first, with continued support in therapy I was able to gain the confidence I needed to begin expressing my true feelings and needs. For the first time in my life I was honoring my wounded child's need to be heard.

Building Self-Esteem and Performing Self-Care

DORIS   As Judy's ability to express her feelings and her needs expanded so did her self-esteem and, in direct correlation, her self-care. Once again, the importance of trust must be acknowledged for trust was also the foundation upon which her personal growth was based; trust that the bonds connecting her with those who continued to support her were solid and trust in the reality of her own perceptions. She could now validate for herself what she saw, heard, and experienced with the knowledge that feedback was available from family and friends.

If she felt any confusion she checked with her therapists. If she disagreed with them she could say so without fear—a new concept for Judy and a risk that she now felt safe enough to take. With each affirmation of the validity of her own perceptions, her self-esteem grew, as did her sense of empowerment. She began to want to expand her horizons, take more risks, and pursue new adventures.

What was, and still is, difficult for Judy is that damage done by the years of abuse, emotionally, psychologically, and physically, continues to take its toll. She must stop many times in the midst of all these exciting new challenges and do some serious self- care. It is sometimes depressing, always frustrating, and absolutely necessary. Whereas in the past her inability to do self-care was a direct reflection of low self-esteem and feelings of unworthiness, her ability to do so now is an indicator that major changes have taken place. Good self-care is now more a conscious expression of a hard-earned belief that she has a right to a healthy and fulfilling life. It is also an expression of her growing autonomy.

JUDY   I was so damaged early in my life, my self-esteem destroyed, that I never experienced feeling good about myself. I never felt special in a good way, I never believed I was loveable, and I never thought I was okay just the way I was. Instead, I was left to feel dirty, ashamed, and worthless. As a result, I was extremely self-critical, self-punishing, and self-abusive. I had no idea there were good things about myself to be loved and nurtured.

To gain any ground on developing self-esteem, I had to first stop the negative internalized messages that ran over and over in my head; messages so destructive they could convince me that I was worse than black pond scum. I began to change that pattern by first being attentive to my feelings. I would ask, "How do you feel about yourself?" If the answer was negative, I would then take action. Cognitively, I would walk myself through a checklist of questions, for instance, "Where did you get that message from?" and "Who might have told you that about yourself before?" Just identifying and discovering the roots of those negative thoughts helped expose the source of the messages. Most of the time, I found that those messages were what I heard from the abusers.

Second, I had to stop believing those messages. When I started to feel bad about myself and I knew they were old messages from my past, I would say to myself, "Stop it. Those thoughts are lies and I don't believe them." This would help affirm that in fact I really didn't feel this way about myself.

Next, I would begin to give positive feedback to myself that I heard from my therapists; messages that were opposite to the negative ones in my head. Using the positive messages I've learned in therapy has helped me parent myself through those rough times.

I also had to learn how to create a positive self-image. I had to stop comparing myself to what I thought was "okay" and accept who I was. To approach these changes I had to first let go of what I thought were other people's expectations of me. I had to see myself as a powerful adult, capable of making positive decisions and goals. As a result, I began to feel a sense of self-respect.

I found that if I obtained a goal that made me feel good, I could also begin to take credit for how hard I worked to make that goal a reality. Consequently, I used this method to improve my self-image which in turn improved my self-esteem. I began to make a mental list of all the things I had accomplished in my life and all the things I found I did well. I included everything I could, for example, "I am a good mother. I am a giving person. I am honest. I am a good artist. I am a survivor. I have accomplished miracles in therapy." As a result of being aware of this list, I began to create an image of myself that I could care about.

Another significant source of healing for my low self-esteem was listening to my spiritual connection within myself. It is the connection to the innocent child, who is worthy of love, respect, and nurturance. It is what Virginia Satir (1985, p. 29) would call, "the treasure inside, called by your name."

Moving through the different stages of post-integration, I found myself moving out of the self-hatred toward feeling proud to have survived what I did. I started to see how far I had come from being a multiple to integrated. I began to understand how much I had accomplished in my life and I began to feel a glimmer of hope for my future. As a result, I began to care for myself better.

I started to care for not only my body, but for my emotional and spiritual needs as well. As a result, I began to build good feelings around taking care of myself, which was in itself a positive reinforcement for this new behavior.

What is most frustrating is having to take time out from my day to rest or take care of myself. The abuse I have suffered has taken its toll on my physical health, which is constantly interrupting my life; I simply don't have the energy resources like other people my age. Yet, there is an appreciation that comes from knowing I have value, and in this way caring for myself is a lovely gift I have given myself.

Using Containment

DORIS   Continuous exposure to triggers that brought up memories and feelings continued to plague Judy's life. Monitoring her environment had proven to be helpful but there was absolutely no way to remove all negative stimuli, nor was it feasible; memories and feelings had to be dealt with if Judy was to complete her work and diminish their intensity. At the same time, she needed to find a way to take control of these painful disturbances in her life so they would not continue to be so disruptive.

The old copings of dissociation and denial no longer fit. By the third stage of post-integration she had learned not to repress the feelings when memories occurred but to express them to her therapists. In this way the intensity was reduced and memories could be dealt with within the safety of the therapeutic setting. However, her therapists were not always handy when such moments arrived and her desire for independence and autonomy had become a strong motivating force.

Here again, the importance of trust was underscored. Judy had learned to trust her own intelligence, her own intuition, and her own judgement. She trusted her "self," and she trusted in the continuing support of her therapists. It was because of trust that she believed that she could do what she wanted to do: Use her cognitive skills to design and implement a method of containment for memories and the accompanying feelings that would give her control as to how and when she would confront them. That she was successful in this is proof that Judy is no longer a captive of her past but an active participant in her present and future.

JUDY   Learning how to use containment was essential to feeling more in charge and in control of my life. This was not only difficult at first, but also challenging. I had to experiment with what fit and what made me comfortable.

I learned that to use containment I needed to use my cognitive skills to go step by step through a procedure of acknowledging my memories and feelings, experiencing my feelings, and then making choices as to when, how, or if I wanted to express those feelings or talk about the memories. If a particular situation triggered feelings or memories of my past, the first thing I would do was acknowledge and validate that I was remembering old stuff. For example, I would say to myself, "Yes, you are remembering what is true and you are safe." I would then identify what feelings I was experiencing and repeat to myself what feeling I had. For example, if I was scared I would say, "Okay Judy, you are feeling afraid." I would then allow that feeling to be a part of me. To keep myself grounded, I would pay attention to my breathing; this kept me in touch with the fact that I wasn't dying just because I was having intense feelings. Next, I would decide what, if anything, I wanted to do with the feelings or memories. Did I want to scream, cry, or hit a pillow? Did I want to just experience the feeling and talk about the memories? Was this something I wanted to share with my therapists or friends?

Most significant was that I could choose to put the feelings and memories away until I found a time I wanted to deal with them. I could contain them simply by acknowledging them and deciding to put them in a safe place until I chose to express them and share them. I no longer had to cut off the feelings from myself or to deny them. As a result, I began to see my range of choices and felt a new sense of personal power. But most important was that I felt a new sense of responsibility for myself because I was in charge.

I was in control and less reactive to the many daily triggers that evoked feelings and memories concerning my past history of abuse. The feelings no longer dominated my behavior. In fact, I was able to recognize the feelings, experience them, and choose what I wanted to do with them. There was no right or wrong way to deal with my feelings. I could sort through and see what I wanted to do with them; I could share them in therapy or with supportive friends; I could find out what was more comfortable for me and see new options in dealing with triggers, feelings, and memories. I was able to contain those feelings without reactive behavior or denial. I was now engaged in an active role of decision making about how I wanted to handle everything about the way I coped with my life; I could choose my own way of dealing with my future.

DORIS   The ability that Judy now had to contain her memories, and to release them and address them at a time of her own choosing gave her the opportunity to "get on with her life" in a more organized manner. Even though there were still daily triggers, the fact that she was able to create a way to handle them changed what would have previously been a reactive response into a gathering of information, information that could be used to diffuse the situation and give Judy some control. Without denying her memories or her feelings she now took charge of how and when they would be addressed.

Taking New Risks and Exploring New Options

DORIS   The confidence Judy was beginning to feel in her own ability to expand her world began to show itself in numerous ways. Now that she was able to contain memories, she had more time to explore and develop the aspects of her life she found truly enjoyable. For the first time Judy's world did not revolve strictly around survival issues, as it had prior to integration. Nor did it revolve around learning how to cope with her new life, as she had done in the first two phases of post-integration. She was now free to explore a very different world, one she had fought all these years to become a part of. She now felt strong enough and safe enough to take the risks that would enable her to take her place in it.

JUDY   For the first time in my life I wasn't waking up in the morning having to face "the work" ahead of me. Instead, I was able to focus on a new day, a new life, new options, and new possibilities. I had the tools and I knew how to use them. Now it was up to me to take the risk of going out into the world to use what I had learned. I was both excited and scared to venture out into unfamiliar territories; I had many expectations, and I was willing to take the risk.

Now, more than ever, I was ready to encounter new life experiences. I began by venturing out, finding creative projects I was interested in. I started to explore new possibilities; possibilities I had dreamed about, but never before tried to accomplish. I became involved in two groups that held a special interest for me, a community-based art group and a Native American cultural awareness group. I also found there was time for self-discovery, making room for new thoughts and beliefs as well as fine-tuning my old skills. I finally had time on my hands, time that belonged to me.

Looking with new eyes and seeing new possibilities did not mean getting rid of all my old coping skills. In fact, I began sorting through my many survival skills, keeping from the past those that remained effective for me as well as adding new skills along the way. As I began to use some of the old skills from the past I realized I could use them in ways that were creative and helpful in the present. For example, I continued to use my observational skills of watching others' behaviors and copying those behaviors if they fit me. In fact, I sought out those people I wanted to use as role models. I remain acutely aware of people's body language and continue to use that skill as a check for congruency.

Most important is that I have awakened not only to myself, but also to my own potential. Now I have the time to explore and sort through all the different, interesting, and exciting things I see around me and develop those areas, both within myself and outside myself, that bring meaning into my life. These new discoveries give my life meaning, a whole new way of being in the world, because I am no longer just trying to fit in; I am finding out what I like, and what I can bring to myself in this world. I am beginning to relate more to the person I am becoming, than to the person I have been. After investing all my time into healing, I have finally reached a point where I can put my energy into living.

Utilizing Dreamwork and Artwork

DORIS   Initially, prior to integration and in our very early sessions, Judy's artwork was that of a child, one of her younger personalities, and the symbols she drew represented the abuse she had suffered. Over time, as older personalities emerged, the artwork became more mature, sometimes specific, sometimes abstract, but always an expression of Judy's inner world. Judy found this artwork to be very useful, not only as a way to express emotions, but also as a useful part of her memory work. In her post-integration work Judy continued to use her art as a way of keeping in touch with that inner world, a world that continues to need expression.

We discovered a correlation between Judy's dreams and her artwork: Both used symbols to express memories and feelings. Dreams proved to be extremely valuable in Judy's progress both before and after integration. We found them to be excellent guides as a means to unraveling the past as well as clarifying the present.

Dreamwork

DORIS   Post-integration in no way diminished Judy's rich and powerful dream life, one that held the answers to many of her questions. It was this dream life that continued to reveal not only the root cause behind any nebulous feelings of fear, anxiety, or depression but that also formed a clear picture of her inner process and the changes that were continually taking place. Through the use of dream symbols, both universal and those uniquely her own, dream interpretation remained a useful tool and an integral part of therapy. Here are some examples from three of her dreams.

Dream One

FIRST SCENE
I am at a lake and a man and woman have a tiny box on wheels which they are pulling behind their car. It is for sale for $200. I have just $200 so I buy it.

DORIS   Prior to integration Judy drew pictures filled with many little boxes, which symbolized her different personalities. In this dream there is only one box and she has just the right amount to make her the owner of the box. Change is shown here not only in the singularity of the box but also in Judy's ability to purchase the box with her own resources; a definite acknowledgement of her own potentiality.

SECOND SCENE
I find out the box is a little portable house, like a tiny trailer. The little portable house is huge inside. There is a bedroom with two beds, a living room with a couch, and a kitchen. The little house smells musty inside, used and old, but that's okay.

DORIS   The box became a house. In Judy's dreams the symbol she uses to represent herself is a house. The "little . . . house" (how it was seen from the outside) proved to be "huge inside." Judy's way of looking at herself is changing. She is beginning to challenge the picture of herself as powerless, exchanging it for one that includes her own extensive inner resources. The fact that this house is not new ("musty") and has been "used" (abused) is an acknowledgement of her personal history; at the same time, "but that's okay" indicates she has accepted that history and herself.

THIRD SCENE
I put the house in my car; I'm going to take it to where my husband is. I'm driving fast, carelessly. "I better slow down."

DORIS   The fear that follows any change is not unexpected. Here Judy reveals an old pattern: "driving fast, carelessly." Endangering herself was one way she relieved the tension of confronting and changing old rules and beliefs. However, in this piece of the dream it is evident that this old pattern is also changing, for she says, "I better slow down"—a sign that even though change still produces anxiety, she is now taking care of herself.

FOURTH SCENE
I have to go through the dumpy part of a big city, which is dirty and trashy. There is a man with a cigar on the sidewalk; he says, "Why don't we fuck sometime?" He says this threateningly because I am female. The man notices I'm female so what he is saying to me is sexual. I say to myself, "You're not scared of him, why don't you just yell at him?" So I do. I am angry and confronting, but not afraid.

DORIS   Judy's being noticed as female has always been a fearful experience. Being noticed meant abuse would soon follow and she would be powerless to stop it. In this part of the dream she is noticed as female and verbally abused in a sexual manner. However, rather than feeling powerless, she responds angrily and without fear. She is powerful.

All four parts of this dream are connected to the changes Judy was experiencing as post-integration therapy continued; learning to live as a singular person, defining, accepting, and implementing her own inner resources. Accepting as natural the fears and anxieties that came with changing old patterns and finding new ways to care for herself through these times and, finally, realizing that in spite of the trash she had to go through (fourth scene), she is no longer in a powerless position and refuses to be victimized.

Dream Two

I am in New York with one of the abusers. We go our separate ways. She lives in a tall skyscraper. There is an earthquake and the building comes down. I go up the steel bars of the remaining part of the building to rescue the abuser and guide her out of the building.

DORIS   This dream clearly reflects the difficulty Judy has had separating from one of her abusers. Changes in this particular relationship resulted in "earthquakes" that, while they might bring down the structure of the relationship, do not completely end the attachment. The strength of that attachment is shown in Judy's need "to rescue the abuser and guide her" to safety. This dream was a reminder of a particularly powerful piece of unfinished business that needed continuing work.

Dream Three

I am going to an art show contest. My painting is small. Another contestant's painting is big. The lady who won the contest had good brushes and finances for her art project. My brushes in comparison are old and tattered. My equipment is not as good.

DORIS   In this dream Judy struggles with self-esteem. She sees herself as not having either the equipment or the materials to compete with others. She is small in comparison to others ("another contestant's painting is big") and Judy does not have the resources ("finances") she needs to be first.

Artwork

DORIS   Since the beginning of therapy Judy was able to express in her art that which she was unable to express in words. It was as powerful a source as her dreams and many times it was an extension. Like her dreams, her art seemed to remove the barriers erected around certain events, and she was able to paint or draw that which was inexpressible otherwise. It was the safest way to examine those parts of her life and an important way to validate her experiences. Post-integration did not end its usefulness. Judy continues to use her art to recover the lost threads of her life as she continues to weave her life together.

JUDY   As a multiple I utilized art as a powerful and effective tool to gain insight into my inner world. I used many styles and forms of art to express not only my damaged feelings and emotions I endured as a result of my childhood, but also the horrendous abuse I suffered. Art allowed me to express in picture-form that which I was unable to verbally express: the hidden worlds of my many personalities, the secrets of the abuse, and the feelings of rage, pain, and confusion.

During my post-integration work I continued to use art to express continuing feelings around the many issues I had left to work on but with this difference: Prior to integration I was using pictographs and symbols to relate information about past abusive events, while trying to put together my dissociated personalities and the stories they represented; after integration my art became more mature, less impulsive, and more reality based. As a result, I began to use my art to express new attitudes and feelings in picture-form even before such changes were tried out in my daily life outside of therapy. In addition, I used my art to resolve conflict, as it served as a catalyst to make change after viewing my art productions.

DORIS   Figure 1 is the drawing of a little girl. Judy brought this drawing into therapy after doing a very difficult piece of work around the feelings of shame, self-blame, and humiliation she still held around issues relating to her abuse. It was during a time in therapy when she was grieving the loss of her inner comforter and guide, the one who could take her to the Shining Place where she

FIGURE 1

felt cared for and accepted even when she was being abused. Now, as she searched for new ways to comfort and accept herself, she realized that the gift she had received from her spiritual guide remained. In her own words:

> The gift that remains from my experience as a child is the belief that I do deserve all the things my child parts experienced while being in the Shining Place. The gift is that I can now see myself as my spiritual part saw me: an injured child; innocent, pure, and loveable. Now I can embrace her.

JUDY   This picture represented for me the intense feelings I was experiencing for the child I once was. By doing this piece of art I found the innocent child I thought I had lost.

DORIS   Figure 2 is a representation of the gathering of Judy's own resources, a powerful expression of post-integration work.

JUDY   I created this picture over a long period of time, from the beginning of post-integration through the final stage of post-integration. It is the representation of the "self" I have found. The nakedness represents the vulnerability I felt born into the world as a newly formed person without the resources of other personalities. As I embrace myself in the picture I am embracing the acceptance of being a singular person, the acceptance of my history, the development of my self-esteem and self-confidence, and the openness to living in the world as an integrated person.

DORIS   Trust had become a powerful resource for Judy and remains at the very center of her expanding ability to make changes and to develop new patterns of coping. The continuing growth of trust in herself and in her own perceptions, has been extremely important. It has allowed her to take the risks necessary to expand her own boundaries and to become more inclusive of others. Trust in her therapists, friends, and family also continues to play a major role in this process. She knows she can trust this select group to give her honest feedback, support, and encouragement. This kind of trust was needed if Judy was ever to learn how to express her feelings and needs, an area that required learning and implementing

FIGURE 2

new skills. Success in reaching desired outcomes strengthened Judy's feelings of self-esteem and thereby reenforced the importance of self-care, especially as a sense of her own worthiness grew.

The ongoing issue of memories is certainly one that continues to burden her, yet it was her ability to retrieve these memories that enabled her to discover the cause of her many difficulties. It was only by getting to the root of her problems that she was able to address all other issues. Learning how to contain these memories has kept her from being overwhelmed and allowed her some control.

Her continued use of dreamwork and artwork are still useful in the expression of her internal struggles as well as her achievements. It is through the use of these mediums that Judy can see how clearly she charts her own course.

chapter 7

Ritual Abuse and the Integrated Multiple

In our first book, *The Family Inside* (Bryant et al., 1992), we discussed the credibility factor of ritual abuse, indicators of ritual abuse, and working with ritually abused multiples. Here we continue our discussion of ritual abuse, with this difference: We will address specifically how ritual abuse and programming continued to affect Judy after integration and how deprogramming was needed to complete the therapy and end her connection to cult programs and indoctrinations.*

DORIS   I began the deprogramming process long before I was fully aware of the magnitude of abuse that had been ritualized. Deprogramming began with the building of trust and safety and progressed to the telling of "secrets."

---

*This chapter is specifically about our work with Judy and will not necessarily apply to other multiples. Though there are many similarities between individuals who suffer from dissociative identity disorder, there are also differences, and all must be taken into consideration when designing a treatment plan.

115

This seemingly basic initial deprogramming was essential to the integration of Judy's many different personalities. Fears around the most fundamental issues of trust, safety, and the revealing of the secrets were all connected to a powerful and terrifying system of beliefs implanted by the abusers and reinforced with continuing abuse.

The result was a carefully crafted program to which other programs were attached over the years, programs specifically designed to reinforce the original program by burying it beneath layer after layer of additional programs; all were connected, yet each was a separate "piece" so designed to keep the entire structure from collapsing if one of the programs were "broken." Therefore, even though the programs that had kept Judy's many personalities separated had been broken and she had achieved unification, some of the hardest work still lay ahead.

JUDY   While I was able to do much of the work around the issues of ritual abuse prior to integration, I found I was still affected after integration by cult programming. Continuing therapy on this particular issue, in fact, was critical not only to my continuing personal development, but also to preserve the gains I had already made throughout post-integration. The most important aspect of this issue was deprogramming—although reframing beliefs, identifying triggers and cues centered around the ritual abuse, coming to terms with this part of my past, and finding new meaning and purpose in life were important as well.

Working on ritual abuse issues during post-integration was dramatically different from working on them during pre-integration. Most significantly, I no longer used dissociation to switch to alter personalities to manage the work in therapy or the posttraumatic stress related to these issues. On the contrary, I was now doing the work myself: remembering the past trauma, talking about its effect on my life, feeling the full intensity of pain from the memories on my own, and making decisions as to how I would deal with these issues. In fact, I believe I could not have done some of the remaining work until after the unification of all my personalities had taken place because some of the memories at this stage were so horrible and emotionally traumatic.

Defining Ritual Abuse

Ritualistic abuse (also called "ritual abuse") is any kind of abuse done in a ceremonial or systematic form by a specific group. The group can be described as a cult or any organized (usually religious) group that performs purposeful rituals that have specific meaning to that organization. Although a child may be abused by one individual in a ritualistic manner, for our purposes we are talking about abuse that occurs in groups. We believe that satanic abuse does occur, and that when you encounter ritual abuse you will more than likely be working with multiples who were involved in satanic cults or their offshoots (Bryant et al., 1992, p. 245).

A more concise definition of ritual abuse was given by the Ritual Abuse Task Force of the Los Angeles County Commission for Women:

> Ritual Abuse is a brutal form of abuse of children, adolescents, and adults, consisting of physical, sexual, and psychological abuse, and involving the use of rituals. Ritual does not necessarily mean satanic. However, most survivors state that they were ritually abused as part of satanic worship for the purpose of indoctrinating them into satanic beliefs and practices. Ritual abuse rarely consists of a single episode. It usually involves repeated abuse over an extended period of time.
>
> The physical abuse is severe, sometimes including torture and killing. The sexual abuse is usually painful, sadistic, and humiliating, intended as a means of gaining dominance over the victim. The psychological abuse is devastating and involves the use of ritual/indoctrination, which includes mind control techniques and mind altering drugs, and ritual/intimidation which conveys to the victim a profound terror of the cult members and of the evil spirits they believe cult members can command. Both during and after the abuse, most victims are in a state of terror, mind control, and dissociation in which disclosure is exceedingly difficult. (Ritual Abuse Task Force, 1991, p. 1)

JUDY   Ritual abuse was the most brutal form of abuse I suffered. I was assaulted at every conceivable level; physically, sexually, psychologically, and spiritually. Through this kind of abuse, the cult gained control of my mind and behaviors when I was a young child. The process they used included dissociation and programming. The purpose was to compel the complete secrecy of cult behaviors and activities, to control my behaviors, and attempt to realign my beliefs to the cult. It was done behind closed doors; in secrecy. It was shrouded by lies and contradictions. It was isolation, fear, intimidation, and physical pain. It was a personal holocaust. Consequently, I remained in a dissociated state of fear and confusion, fatigued beyond description, believing that my very thoughts and feelings, in fact my very soul, were controlled by the cult. And because I was able to use dissociation, and to split and develop multiple personalities, I survived.

DORIS   I often think that children who survive ritual abuse and grow up into adults are walking miracles. Not able to draw help from their outside environment, they create an inner environment that enables them to survive the most heinous of crimes.

It was Judy's powerful drive to survive that was the strength of her work in therapy. It was this strength that made it possible for her to continue with the difficult work that still lay ahead — strength to face not only the reality of the extent of the abuse, but also the horror engendered as she faced a greater reality: The abuse had happened to her.

During the integrative process it had been impossible to avoid confronting the facts of her abuse as the inner system opened up and the secrets were told, but it had been a "shared" experience. Now she was on her own. Just as it had taken unbelievable courage for each personality to tell of the events that had led to the creation of the "inner family," the same kind of courage would be demanded of Judy as she continued with not only post-integrative work, but the extremely difficult and frightening work of dismantling the deeply embedded programs.

Programming and Indoctrination

DORIS   Programming in its most benevolent form begins for all of us at an early age. Injunctions such as "Don't touch" and "Say thank you," frequently used with toddlers, are very early programmings about acceptable behaviors and depending upon the child's response earn either approval or disapproval from the primary caretakers and are either rewarded or rebuked. That we encounter programming in its more innocuous form every day, even participate in it, is evidenced by the number of parents who find themselves buying "designer" apparel for their children. I use these examples to point out that "programming" need not be a pernicious term. However, in this chapter we are not talking about a benevolent form of programming, but about programming at its most malevolent: programs designed to achieve total control over another human being for the purpose of using that human being in any manner the programmer sees fit.

Dr. Walter Young (1992) describes programming as follows:

> A "program" is a highly complex and specific indoctrinated stimulus/response pattern which has been instilled and then reinforced through repeated trauma by cult members. "Indoctrination" is the broader training process of inducing the programming itself, without specificity as to content. The environment for indoctrination is most conducive when there is low resistance, impaired reality, and limited availability of cognitive discrimination because of the effects of factors such as torture, fatigue, the use of drugs, intimidation, fear hyperstimulation, and sensory deprivation. (p. 273)

Young also explains the difference between triggers and cues:

> A "trigger" is any generalized stimulus that produces an intense and irrational emotional response. The triggering event or vehicle may or may not be directly related to the patient's experience. Triggers can be so pervasive and intense that they can seriously impair the patient's ability to function in the world, whereas, a "cue" is a specific conditioned stimulus or message intended to elicit a specific programmed reaction. Unlike triggers, cues are reportedly deliberate and have been programmed into the individual, sometimes years or even decades earlier. (p. 274)

Neswald, Gould, and Graham-Costain (1991) state:

All programs are stimulus-sensate triggered. Thus, programs
may be enacted (triggered) via auditory, visual, tactile, olfac-
tory and/or gustatory modalities. Classical, operant, and obser-
vational/modeling paradigms all are utilized by the cults and
their "programmers." Finally, it is important to note that virtu-
ally all cult programs will possess a variety of secondary and
tertiary back-ups, perhaps several layers of each. (p. 47)

From a systemic point of view, it makes sense that a multiple
who was ritually abused will have one or more personalities who
were created to carry out assigned roles in the cult. These personalities will continue to be a part of the inner family system, even
if the adult is no longer involved in the cult. The inner system
remains set up *as if* the cult still existed in her life. And if the
multiple was programmed at one time as part of the ritual abuse
(which is almost a certainty), the program may still be actively working to either keep the client in contact with the cult or to keep the
client feeling as if she were still in contact with the cult even when
she is not. She will have the same fears and responses to programmed stimuli, even if she is not actively involved with the cult
at present.

Cult programs can include self-injury programs, such as cutting
or burning, which condition the victim to routinely injure oneself;
suicide programs, instructing a survivor when and how they should
attempt to kill themselves, particularly if damaging material to the
cult is disclosed or when the cult feels it has lost all other forms of
control of the victim; and reporting programs, in which the victim is
conditioned to routinely contact and report back to the cult (Neswald et al., 1991).

Cult programming can also include interference programming,
such as scrambling programs intended to confuse and disorganize
the victim's memories, thought processes, and/or incoming information, and nightmare/night-terror programs in which the victim is
overwhelmed with terrifying images/memories while asleep. Such
programs are deeply ingrained and appear to be primarily used for
punishment. They serve to keep the patient run-down and fatigued
(Neswald et al., 1991).

In addition, cults focus their initial efforts most frequently and strenuously on achieving mind control with children under the age of six. Like developmental psychologists, cult programmers understand that people are most susceptible to having their character, beliefs, and behavior molded during this early period of development. Catherine Gould (1992) concludes,

> These forms of abuse are perpetrated by a cult in a highly systematic way, utilizing ceremonies and symbols, in an attempt to indoctrinate the victim into the cult's antisocial, life-destructive belief system. . . . Through an elaborate process of abuse and indoctrination, the cult attempts to gain absolute control over their victims' minds in order to transform them into members who will function in whatever way the cult demands. To forge a new member who is maximally useful to the cult, the process of abuse and indoctrination must begin when the child is very young. (p. 207)

DORIS   Since Judy had grown up being controlled and indoctrinated in a cult environment, we knew that the deprogramming would require us to seek out each program and then dismantle it piece by piece. We had already removed some of those pieces prior to integration but comparatively speaking we'd just done the "easy" part.

We had found that all programs appeared to be connected to one major program, one that had been implanted at an early age; each successive program was attached to that one. All abuse prior to the implanting of that program was but a preparation for that one program and all abuse after was designed to keep that program firmly in place and reinforce the cult's indoctrination.

JUDY   My experience of cult programming began in my early childhood, before the age of three. I was terrorized and physically abused until I created a split-off part of myself. The abusers then manipulated my dissociated response with intolerable pain. When I was maximally dissociated the abusers would instruct the split-off part, or personality, about what function she would have. For example, a split-off part would be instructed to be harmful to myself or others and would be programmed to activate when cued. Then, that part was given a cue word as a name, such as "cutter," so she could be called out by the abusers at will or activated by triggers outside the cult. The part of my body that had been abused, like my feet or hands, was now associated with a particular personality so when that particular part of my body was touched, that personality would be activated.

What was different after integration was that I no longer had alter personalities that were programmed, but, instead, programs that remained repressed and were still capable of being triggered with the proper cue or stimulus. In other words, I was no longer a multiple experiencing the effects of cult programming, but a whole integrated self still being affected by stimulus/response patterns.

DORIS   The continuing impact of the cult environment which had involved Judy in ritual abuse could not be denied. Triggers and cues connected to deeply embedded programs continued to disrupt her life. Even though we had successfully unraveled program after program during the integration process and had continued to do so after integration, we had yet to reach the main program. The realization that her work with deprogramming was far from finished filled Judy with despair.

JUDY   Following integration and after accomplishing a substantial amount of work on deprogramming, I was devastated to find I was still experiencing specific behaviors triggered by programs set in place by my abusers during my childhood. It seemed as if there was an endless maze of undefined work that still lay ahead. There were times I just couldn't believe there was still more work to be done, yet the reality was that there were times I remained terrorized with post-traumatic stress—terrorized by the belief that the cult could still manipulate me, and by the continuing memories of horrendous abuse. More importantly, I was afraid the remaining effects of ritual abuse would diminish both my capacity to function in the way I had been functioning and the progress I had gained in both pre- and post-integration therapy.

Meanwhile, what remained to be worked on were indoctrinated beliefs and programs of the cult and at times I thought my nightmare of ritual abuse and my feelings of guilt would never end, and my continuing behaviors could never be changed. My gut was tied in knots as I considered the implications of having to do more work in post-integration around issues of ritual abuse. It felt as if there was still yet another wall standing in my way; one so tall, I wondered at times if it could keep me from reaching the freedom I so much deserved.

Working on the remaining cult programs always felt as if I were taking four steps backwards. It often interrupted the flow of work in post-integration therapy, moving my therapy from individual growth work to where my only focus was on ritual abuse issues. In addition, it sometimes challenged the work I had previously done in therapy, bringing up conflicting feelings and thoughts; feelings and thoughts I had previously resolved around issues of trust and safety, self-esteem, personal power, and trusting my own perceptions. I felt confused having to challenge and resolve these once again.

Though disappointed and depressed, I also felt angry when the need to work on another ritual abuse issue arose. In fact, I was furious. And it was this anger that gave me the energy I needed to continue the work. I had worked so long and so hard in therapy to get to were I was that I was not going to let just one more program stand in my way. For this purpose, I allowed myself to use my anger as an energy source to move beyond the depression into action. The anger, in fact, was exactly what allowed me to get the information from the inside to the outside and allow the healing to begin.

Treatment and Deprogramming

DORIS   "I had discovered during Judy's integration process that she had developed a very distinctive coping cycle.* Post-integration, during deprogramming, Judy, Lynda,† and I discovered that there was also a pattern to the work in process and this pattern also had

*See Bryant et al., 1992, p. 169–186.
†Lynda Shirar, cotherapist.

very definite phases. This was extremely helpful to us for the element of surprise was removed and we could determine the progress of the deprogramming by the outcomes and behaviors that accompanied each phase. It was also helpful to Judy; although it did not rid her of the chaos, it at least provided her with understanding of the process and a structure within which she could complete her work.

Following are the different phases Judy experienced each time a program was triggered (trigger unknown) and then removed.

Phase 1: Denial
Outcomes: Deny, Minimize, Distract

JUDY   During my years of therapy I learned what my personal signals were that indicated a cult program was about to surface. Clearly, I felt discouraged every time they appeared in therapy or as they began to disrupt my life. I would fight both myself and the therapy to keep from having to face the reality of yet another memory of ritual abuse. I would deny, minimize, and distract my feelings, trying hard to keep the memories, even the signals, from surfacing. But, I could not hold them back. The signals became too clear and the memories too overwhelming. The feelings of rage, confusion, and even disappointment festered inside.

DORIS   This phase could last for several weeks or more while Judy would busy herself with many activities in an attempt to repress an emerging program. She would struggle to maintain a calm demeanor in therapy, a demeanor which was belied by her body language and her increasing sensitivity.

It was during this initial phase that a word spoken by either one of her therapists, either in conversation or in discussing one of her dreams, that something that was said would act as a trigger and Judy would go automatically into a trance. Since this was the state in which the cue was implanted we knew that a program was beginning to surface. Sometimes, in this state, Judy would reveal one of the cues but later would not remember she had done so.

Phase 2: Confusion
Outcomes: Mistrust of Therapists,
Irrational Thoughts, Increasing Confusion

JUDY   The first apparent indication that I was beginning to have trouble with a ritual abuse issue was my feeling of mistrust toward my therapists. Confusion overwhelmed my cognitive skills. On the one hand, I knew I had an open, trusting relationship with my therapists but on the other hand I felt like I couldn't trust them. This made me feel disoriented and jumbled inside. I could not, at this point, clearly think through what was happening to me. My feelings overpowered my rational behaviors.

I would question my therapists' motives, asking them, "Why do you want to know that?" I would question their behaviors, asking, "Why did you look at me like that?" And I would question their questions, all the while my anxiety escalating into fear. "My God," I thought, "What is happening to me?"

By this time, I was sweating, fidgeting, and doing whatever I could to distract myself and my therapists; trying to keep the focus of our conversation off of me. I became less willing to participate in the therapy, less talkative — even secretive, hiding my thoughts and feelings from my therapists, wishing, even, to hide myself. Spinning with confusion, the feeling of shame took over while chaos seemed to inundate the sessions.

DORIS   This phase was particularly confusing for Judy for it was during this phase that the powerful injunction "Don't trust, don't tell" came to the foreground with feelings so intense that all cognitive learnings were thrown into disarray.

We knew that this injunction, which was attached to every program, brought with it the terrifying threat of reprisals if there was ever any revealing of "the secrets." It was only because of the previous work done in therapy around the issues of trust and safety that Judy could "hear" that her therapists were aware of her confusion and fears and understood her dilemma even though, paradoxically, this was what she was trying to hide.

The therapy sessions were centered around reaffirming trust and safety issues and using dreamwork, artwork, and the sand tray to begin work on the bits and pieces of the program that were ready to come to the surface.

Pressure to "get to the program" was never an option. Judy was highly motivated to change her life and followed her own internal guide in these matters. Pressure to move more quickly or explore more deeply would have the reverse effect of blocking the flow of energy needed to do the work and causing confusion and fear by triggering old beliefs such as "I'm not doing it the right way" or "I can't think for myself."

It was absolutely necessary during any deprogramming to move slowly with Judy through these difficult times, affirming the reality of the bits and pieces of information as they surfaced and adding information of our own when appropriate. Within the safety of such an environment we were able to begin the dismantling of the program.

Phase 3: Memories and Feelings
Outcomes: Anxiety Attacks,
Body Memories, Nighttime Terrors,
Insomnia, Exhaustion

JUDY   While therapy seemed to be breaking down, so did my ability to manage my life at home. I was certainly having the worst time outside of therapy. I became withdrawn, depressed, and ex-hausted from trying to hold myself together. Consequently, holding onto the denial that a program was not surfacing was now nearly impossible. I began to experience more anxiety attacks and body memories. And by the time I resigned myself to the fact there was a cult program surfacing, my life had become totally disrupted.

Sleeping through the night became impossible. Waking with cold sweats was a common occurrence. While the worst was yet to come, the nighttime fear was so deep within my soul I could neither call out for help nor move my body out of the position it was in. I became immobilized with terror.

My feelings of anxiety were replaced by fear while my reactions dissolved into panic to such a degree that I felt a need to isolate myself from any and all stimulation or interaction. The intensity of feelings was too overwhelming. This stage was difficult and painful; I became more and more disorganized, less able to cope with the stress, and more likely to escalate into a crisis.

DORIS   During this phase Judy resisted therapy, but it was important that she maintain contact with her therapists for she needed the reassurance that she would not be abandoned at this crucial time. She had now reached the point where a program was just below the surface, ready to emerge and with such force that it was rather like a volcano on the verge of eruption. Not only must she combat the fears in her everyday life, but also the fear of what this eruption would bring forth.

More bits and pieces of the program were revealed to Judy's conscious mind in therapy, while much of what lay in the unconscious was revealed in her dreams or in self-induced trance-like states. Some of the material she received in these trance-like states she remembered immediately, other pieces of information came into her conscious awareness only gradually and over a period of time. Records kept of the sessions were invaluable to Judy when she sought answers to what had transpired during those missing intervals. Her dreams also provided a rich body of information regarding both the process and the progress of her work.

JUDY   My dream life has always been one of my most powerful resources in therapy and I would usually have several dreams, which I had written down, to bring to each therapy session. Clearly within my dreams there were symbols I had become accustomed to seeing as indicators of ritual abuse, for example, sharks, locked doors hidden beneath deep oceans or bodies of water, and seeing myself fly through the air. The following is a dream I brought to therapy, showing ritual abuse symbols and indicating a program was surfacing.

There is a large, wood, old, two-story house, way, way out in a very isolated part of the country. The only way to the house is on a small motorboat down these waterways. There are hundreds of these waterways, filled with sharks and alligators. The water is very dark, murky, and mossy.

My husband drives us from the house to a dock. He leaves and goes to work. I have forgotten to remember the way back to the house. I'm afraid. I don't know how to drive the boat. My husband shows me. I try and almost sink the boat. It fills up with water. I'm scared of the sharks and alligators in the water.

DORIS   In Judy's dreams, old houses symbolize her "old self." It was in this "old self" where the cult programs had been stored in an isolated part that was very difficult to reach. To find her way back to the programs' source required her to navigate through the "hundreds of . . . waterways filled with sharks and alligators," that is, her memories of ritual abuse and back-up programs meant to keep her from reaching her destination.

In therapy Judy had been preparing herself to confront the past and her dream reveals she knows the way back to the "house," as shown by a cognitive part, but she has "forgotten to remember," not only because she is terrified of what will happen if she should reach her destination but also because back-up programs of "don't tell" are still in place. She doesn't know "how to drive the boat," the vehicle that would keep her safely afloat over that which is lurking in the murkiness of her unconscious. Once again her cognitive part shows the way, but she cannot keep from taking on the unconscious material and is fearful that memories and feelings will overwhelm and engulf her, and she will be lost.

As with all of Judy's dreams, this dream proved to be very useful in therapy. Its familiar symbols clearly showed her that she was indeed coping with ritual abuse issues. The fact that the dream was a message from herself to herself and wasn't coming from her therapists also played a major role in her ability to confront her own denial. The dream also pointed out that she *did* know how to get to the program in spite of her many fears.

Phase 4: Abreaction and Depression
Outcomes: Flooding of Memories,
Withdrawal, Overwhelming Feelings,
Removing the Program

DORIS   The dream we have previously discussed reveals that for Judy there was a part of herself who could guide us through the many labyrinths of back-up programs. This inner guide, who proved to be a constant during the deprogramming work, seemed to support and validate Judy's right to seek out the program as if in anticipation of the conflicts that lay ahead—for once the major body of the work began, the impetus to remove that program would increase in intensity and Judy would be flooded with memories, feelings, and fears.

JUDY   I found this phase very difficult for I was working on the bits and pieces of information that continued to surface from memories and dreams, trying to put them into some believable context. Just as important, I had to come to terms with the experiences I had remembered. Bit by bit more information surfaced, although most of the time it was disconnected and fragmented.

As I continued to use my dreams, journaling, and artwork, the dissociative barriers began to dissolve. At times the dissociative barriers would dissolve rapidly and a massive breakthrough of memory would occur. Either way, this stage was extremely painful. So many feelings would rush to the surface that I felt overwhelmed trying to assimilate the new information. Spiraling down into a deep depression, I truly believed I did not deserve continued therapy, I did not deserve to live, and I should be punished for my participation in the cult. I felt dirty, ugly, and ashamed.

DORIS   It was during this phase that Judy gathered up all the pieces of the program. As she fit each one with the next a clear picture emerged for her of the event during which the program had been implanted and the words that had been employed to cue the program. Her feelings and her memories were no longer a terrifying jumble; she could see they were connected to a whole experience and understand for the first time the source of that jumble. This knowledge brought an end to that program, but the cost was high for Judy. Each time a program was removed she reexperienced and relived the horror of that time and would be overcome with grief as she accepted how desperately a little child fought to live and acknowledged that child as herself.

JUDY   Deprogramming was similar to the abreactive/memory work I had done to integrate my alter personalities. It meant I had to remember what actually happened to me during the abuse. I had to feel emotionally what feelings I had during the abuse, expressing and experiencing them with the same intensity. I had to identify and experience the body trauma caused by the abuse. I had to understand and acknowledge the meaning of the abusive event. And last, I had to find "the actual words" said by the cult programmers in order to process them and discuss their meaning within therapy.

Abreacting the memories, piecing them together, and deprogramming was an arduous task and I was left feeling physically and emotionally drained after the work. Inundated with feelings of grief and loss I was again overwhelmed with depression.

Phase 5: Resolution
Outcomes: Reconnection and Grief

DORIS   Once a program was removed, so too was the chaos and the confusion under which Judy had struggled to maintain some semblance of an orderly everyday life. No longer overwhelmed by feelings, she could then acknowledge the importance of the work she had done and reconnect with her usual appreciation for life, her family, and her friends. During this time she also regained a sense of security with her therapists, reconnecting with the knowledge that she could trust them. This was very important, for during this resolution period she needed a place where she could safely recount the remembered horrors and grieve her losses, and Judy did not wish to disturb her home environment by discussing with family members the memories of the dreaded events that had occurred in her life. So it was within the therapeutic setting that tears, anger, and sorrow were released and she was able to resolve her grief.

JUDY   Although I felt engulfed by depression, I knew I would have to move toward honoring my pain, expressing my feelings, and accepting my memories. Once I was able to fully express the feelings of grief, a transformation would begin to take place. Grieving became a great relief.

What helped me the most in therapy at this time was my therapists' strong and continued support, their explanations to clarify information, and their validation of my feelings, while at the same time reframing my mixed-up beliefs. With an unfailing steadfast-ness, my therapists helped me to understand that as a child I was the victim; I was manipulated and I had been controlled by the adults in my life; and that the beliefs that I should die, that I was responsible, and that I was shameful were learned while under extreme fatigue, abuse, overstimulation, and deprivation—that, in fact, they were lies intended for the cult's purpose.

As I worked through my grief, and once again connected with my therapists, I felt safe in therapy, trusting the guidance they offered, and experiencing an honest, open relationship, and I began to affirm my strengths and recognize my resiliency. I was living once more with an appreciation of my deep desire to be heathy.

Epilogue

For all these years
you've protected
the seed.
It's time to become
the flower.

Stephen C. Paul

JUDY   There is no such thing as absolute healing. I can never erase my history. The abuse happened. It affected me in profound ways. That will never change. But I have reached a new beginning, a starting place. I have come to terms with my future.

I have met the needs of the seedling and like the seed I have begun to grow. I will blossom, not in my youth, but in the autumn of my life. I have been touched by grace, fascinated and moved by my creation of wholeness, and energized by the power of new growth. My body, mind, and spirit have been renewed. I have experienced the miracle of birth. I am the flower.

References

Bryant, D., Kessler, J., & Shirar, L. (1992). *The family inside: Working with the multiple.* New York: Norton.

Braun, B. (1985). The transgenerational incidence of dissociation and multiple personality disorder: A preliminary report. In R. Kluft (Ed.), *Childhood antecedents of multiple personality disorder* (pp. 127–150). Washington, DC: American Psychiatric Press.

Clarke, J. (1978). *Self-esteem: A family affair.* Minneapolis, MN: Winston Press.

Erikson, E. (1950). *Childhood and society.* New York: Norton.

Gould, C. (1992). Diagnosis and treatment of ritually abused children. In S. Devine and D. Sakheim (Eds.), *Out of darkness: Exploring satanism & ritual abuse* (pp. 207–248). New York: Lexington.

Greaves, G. B. (1989). Precursors of integration in the treatment of multiple personality disorder: Clinical reflections. *Dissociation, 2*(4), 224–23.

Hocking, S. (1992). *Living with your selves: A survival manual for people with multiple personalities.* Rockville: Launch Press.

Kluft, R. (1985). Using hypnotic inquiry protocols to monitor treatment progress and stability in MPD. *American Journal of Clinical Hypnosis, 28,* 63–75.

Kluft, R. (1986). Treating children who have multiple personality disorder. In B. Braun (Ed.), *Treatment of multiple personality disorder* (pp. 81–105). Washington, DC: American Psychiatric Press.

Kluft, R. (1988). The post-unification treatment of multiple personality disorder: First findings. *American Journal of Clinical Psychiatry, 42,* 212–228.

Kübler-Ross, E. (1975). *Death: The final stage of growth.* New York: Simon & Schuster.

Neswald, D., Gould, C., & Graham-Costain, V. (1991, September/October). Common "programs" observed in survivors of satanic riualistic abuse. *The California Therapist,* 47–50.

O'Regan, B. (Ed.). (1985). *Investigations,* 1(3/4), 1–23.

Putnam, F., Guroff, J., Silberman, E., Barban, L., & Post, R. (1986). The clinical phenomenology of multiple personality disorder: Review of 100 cases. *Journal of Clinical Psychiatry, 47,* 285–293.

Putnam, F. (1989). *Diagnosis and treatment of multiple personality disorder.* New York: Guilford.

Ritual Abuse Task Force, Los Angeles County Commission for Women. (1991). *Ritual abuse: Definition, glossary, and the use of mind control.* Los Angeles: Author.

Satir, V. (1978). *Your many faces: The first step to being loved.* Berkeley: Celestial Arts.

Satir, V. (1985). *Virginia Satir: Meditations & inspirations.* Berkeley: Celestial Arts.

Young, W. (1992). Recognition and treatment of survivors reporting ritual abuse. In S. Devine and D. Sakheim (Eds.), *Out of darkness: Exploring satanism & ritual abuse* (pp. 249–278). New York: Lexington.

Index